The Theory of Power and Organization

The Theory of Power and Organization

Stewart Clegg

School of Humanities
Griffith University, Brisbane

Routledge & Kegan Paul
London, Boston and Henley

First published in 1979
by Routledge & Kegan Paul Ltd

39 Store Street,
London WC1E 7DD,
Broadway House,
Newtown Road,
Henley-on-Thames,
Oxon RG9 1EN and
9 Park Street,
Boston, Mass. 02108, USA

Photoset in 10 on 12 Compugraphic Times English by
Kelly and Wright, Bradford-on-Avon, Wiltshire
and printed in Great Britain by
Redwood Burn Ltd,
Trowbridge and Esher

British Library Cataloguing in Publication Data

Clegg, Stewart
The theory of power and organization.
1. Power (Social sciences)   2. Organization
I. Title
301.15'52   HM131   78–41161

ISBN 0 7100 0143 6

Contents

Preface

In April 1975 I began work as the first European Group for Organization Studies (EGOS) Research Fellow. My brief was to conduct research into recent European work on the theory of power, with particular reference to the analysis of organizations. This book is the result of that enquiry, which I completed a little more than two years later, by which time I was no longer the EGOS Fellow, but a lecturer in the School of Humanities at Griffith University, Brisbane, Australia. Between the two jobs there stretch not only two years and half the world, but also the gap between a community of scholars primarily involved in the analysis of organizations and one primarily involved in the discourse of the humanities. That gap is reflected in the terrain of this study.

I had trodden some of this ground previously, in a preparatory way, in my work on *Power, Rule and Domination* (Clegg, 1975). On that occasion the enquiry was cast primarily in terms of the definition, clarification and critique of concepts and the frameworks in which they had been used, in order to provide a focus for empirical enquiry into conversational materials collected on a construction site. In some respects the focus of that work was rather more on the analysis and critique of frameworks of enquiry, such as behaviourism, positivism, ethnomethodology and various forms of relativistic and nihilistic enquiry, than it was on power. Such is not the case with this work.

Beginning work on this project was something I approached with mixed feelings. Since completing *Power, Rule and Domination* I had spent some time lecturing at Trent Polytechnic, Nottingham, and had not had much chance or occasion to re-think those issues which had preoccupied me when I was writing the earlier work. So the ground that I was to research was not unfamiliar to me—indeed, I initially wondered if it might not be too familiar. I had not reckoned on how little I had scratched the surface. This soon became evident to me as I began to accumulate a much wider bibliography than I had previously gathered. In addition, new and important contributions such as that of Steven Lukes (1974) were published shortly after I had completed my earlier work.

It seemed to me that, understandable as it was that EGOS should have stipulated an emphasis on the 'European' aspect of my work, there was not much sense in a strictly territorial division of an intellectual field, particularly one which hardly existed in any coherent way. This latter fact was most apparent from an EGOS Symposium on Power that I organized in May 1976 as part of my Fellowship activities. Among the people who attended, from various branches of the social sciences throughout Western Europe, there was very little unity of either perspective or problems. While some people had much to say about power in the abstract, they had much less to say about power as it applied to organizations as a field of study. The reverse was just as true. Many of the people who were talking about organizations had very little to say about the concepts of power that the 'power people' were discussing. It must have been a little confusing at times for some of the participants.

The first chapter attempts to locate and deal with some of the causes of this confusion by considering the ways in which one might organize a critical enquiry into a terrain whose rules of functioning are presumed to be Europe, power and organizations. It does this by estranging the topics of its discourse as an opening gambit of critical enquiry. Thus, it makes problematic the concepts of Europe, power and organization, as a preliminary to critique of the concept of sociology as a meta-discourse.

This second chapter, 'Method and sociological discourse', prepares the overall framework in which the enquiry is conducted, by elaborating what I took at the time that I wrote this chapter (which was much nearer my earlier work (Clegg, 1976) than the other chapters) to be an adequate method of critical enquiry into discourse. This method is then applied in the remaining chapters, beginning in chapter 3 with an analysis of Hobbes' work on power, in order to fix what become the ideological parameters of subsequent enquiry. These are explored in an extensive analysis of contemporary political, organization and administrative science.

The fourth chapter focuses specifically on what has become the single most contested ground of enquiry into power: the debate generated by the various contributions of Bachrach and Baratz (1962; 1970) and regenerated by the publication of Lukes' (1974) *Power: A Radical View*, and developed in the work of Terence Ball (1975; 1976). This chapter deals in detail with this debate because it is of central importance in the attempt to develop a linked theory of power and structure. Any such theory is crucial for the analysis of power in organizations. I conclude that Lukes' attempt to provide such a linkage is not entirely satisfactory, precisely because his vocabulary and grammar of theorizing remain trapped in the ideological fictions of Hobbes, and because of contradictions engendered when such a discourse is stretched to deal with social structure.

A number of attempts have been made by theorists who locate themselves outside the identifiable mainstream of enquiry into power to link the concepts of power and structure. The most notable of these theorists would be Talcott Parsons. Parsons' work has generated one extremely important criticism for any analysis of power, that of Anthony Giddens (1968). Chapter 5 begins by considering Parsons' (collected in Parsons, 1967) work on power, Giddens' (1968) critique of it and concludes by considering Giddens' (1976) most recent attempt to link power and structure in his *New Rules of Sociological Method*. In this work the attempted linkage is made through a synthesis of action and structure, meaning and power, phenomenology and Marx. It is arguable that in the process of this synthesis Marx receives scant scrutiny compared with phenomenology, and that one result of this is that, just as in Lukes, structure is once again made to flow from action, to the detriment of attempts at structural analysis of power.

These issues of contemporary Marxist analysis are the terrain of chapter 6, which deals in passing with the work of Nicos Poulantzas (1973) and specifically with the work of Antonio Gramsci (1971), with particular reference to the concepts of a mode of production and hegemony. These concepts are linked to the discussion of power and structure (with particular reference to organization structures) via a consideration of the role of the intellectuals.

Chapter 7 attempts a reconceptualization of some key notions of system and structure with respect to organizations. This chapter attempts to develop a more structural analysis of power than that accomplished with the concepts of the earlier chapters. It draws on the ideas of Gramsci discussed in the previous chapter. The notion of system is reconceptualized after the work of Wallerstein (1974a), not at the level of the organization but at the level of the environment. The notion of structure is reconceptualized after the work of Offe (1972; 1976). An abstract model of the organization structure is proposed, which it is envisaged may be of some use in conducting comparative historical research into organizations as they have developed empirically. No such empirical work is

Preface

attempted in this short book, as it is beyond the scope of this present theoretical study. However, it is hoped to be able to report on some empirical application of the model in future work. In this volume the construction of the model of the organization as a structure of sedimented selection rules is proposed and illustrated with some historical examples, in order to construct an abstract and idealized mode of rationality of organizational development. This allows me to reconsider the historical basis of some organization theories of power in such a way that their historical specificity is used to question their general utility. From this reconsideration a general theory of power, control and structure in organizations is suggested.

I would like to acknowledge the generous encouragement of my colleagues in EGOS, especially Jean de Kervasdoué, Elina Almasy, Franco Ferraresi, Walter Goldberg, David Hickson, Lucien Karpik, Jean-Pierre Vignolle, Arthur Wassenberg, Arthur McCullough, David Dunkerley, Tony Spybey and David Wilson for the friendship, support and advice that they have offered me. Above all, David Silverman has been a good friend and critic. In addition, I would like to thank the participants in the EGOS Symposium on Power held at Bradford University in May 1976; my students in the first-semester course on Power and Organizations at Griffith University in 1977; and the various bodies from whom I have received generous financial assistance: the International Institute of Management in Berlin, the Thyssen Foundation in Köln, and the Maison des Sciences de l'Homme in Paris. Bradford University generously allowed me to use their facilities as a visiting scholar in order to have a base from which to conduct my research.

The figure on page 2 and the table on page 3 are reproduced with permission from the 'Introduction: European versus American Organization Theories' by M. Sami Kassem, in *European Contributions to Organization Theory*, edited by Geert Hofstede and M. Sami Kassem, published by Van Gorcum, Assen/Amsterdam, The Netherlands.

Chapter 2 is a revised version of my contribution to *The Social Contexts of Method*, edited by Michael Brenner, Peter Marsh and Marylin Brenner, published by Croom Helm, London and St Martin's Press, New York.

One acknowledgment stands above all others and that is to Lynne Clegg, to whom the work is dedicated.

Stewart Clegg,
Brisbane

x

Chapter 1
Method: critical enquiry into concepts?

The task with which I began this work was to conduct a critical analysis of recent European work on power in organization theory. The field seemed quite specific: 'Europe', 'power' and 'organization theory'—three totalities among which one must constitute connections, 'critically'. Yet to be 'critical' would immediately demand suspending one's reliance on such seemingly factitious entities as a socio-political and geographic area, a topic of discourse, and a means of organizing that discourse. By what criteria is one to isolate these phenomena? What is 'European'? Is it the Europe of the Economic Community, NATO, the Cold War? Or is it an historical Europe, of the nineteenth century perhaps? And if so, does one include the Balkans and Russia? On geographical criteria, possibly. But what weight do we attach to geographical criteria when we are dealing with intellectual formations? Perhaps 'Europe' refers not to a geographical area at all, but to a political and cultural division of the universe. So we might be tempted to regard it as a metaphor for a definite social formation—the area of Europe not under Soviet hegemony. But this might be more accurately regarded, on closer inspection, as a social formation only by pressure of externally conceived forces; it may have no valid unity of its own in anything other than the most expedient and frail terms.

Possibly, then, our conception has to be less static: we must seek for a Europe embedded in something more fluid than a definite space and time—the development of European 'thought' perhaps? But how would we determine the boundaries of this? Once, when its parameters were staked in the Enlightenment, or in the progression of an idea of critical reason as it developed from Kant, this might have been possible. But no such harmony of dialogue unites knowledge now, if indeed it ever did. And European 'thought', in this sense, may now be equated with the entire rationalist project which conceives of science as the only valid knowledge. What, in this almost global project, is definitively European? In short, the task may be impossible to delineate in any

1

valid way, other than through some exclusion rules whose function would only be admissible in constituting a framework that would function in either a purely chauvinist or ideological fashion. This would present a framework within which one might expect only a partial, distorted and uncritical enquiry could flourish.

Elsewhere, I have argued that 'a distinctively European tradition is emergent' (Clegg and Dunkerley, 1977, p. 2). Nor is this the only attempt to distinguish that which is specifically 'European' in organization theory. Kassem (1976b, p. 7) has attempted to formulate the 'distinctiveness' of European, as opposed to American, organization theory, as shown in figure 1.

Figure 1 A scheme for thinking about organization theory: European and American styles (from Kassem, 1976b)

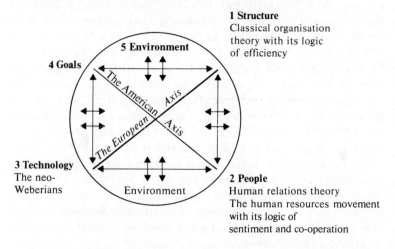

1 Structure
Classical organisation theory with its logic of efficiency

5 Environment

4 Goals

The American Axis

The European Axis

3 Technology
The neo-Weberians

Environment

2 People
Human relations theory
The human resources movement with its logic of sentiment and co-operation

Kassem (1976a) distinguishes the respective emphases in terms of an American stress on 'people' and 'goals', identified by the axis 2–4, and a European emphasis (axis 1–3) which stresses 'structure' and 'technology'. He also notes that, on the whole, European scholars have been 'more concerned with identity and power than their American colleagues' (Kassem, 1976b, p. 12). Kassem maintains that 'power is [an] issue of central concern to European theorists. It is a recurring theme in the writings of Crozier (U.S.A., 1973), Emery and Thorsrud (1969, 1975), Herbst (1962, 1974), Hjelholt (1972), Mayntz and Scharpf (1975), and Mulder (1971, 1974). Unlike most of their American counterparts, these writers hit the issue of power head on' (Kassem, 1976a, p. 54). However,

Kassem qualifies his remarks apropos American organization theory, in that the ' "American sociological school", which includes Merton, Gouldner, Dubin, Blau and Scott, and Etzioni, among others, offers a somewhat different picture; and much of the comparison between the United States and Europe applies less to them' (Kassem, 1976b, p. 56). He summarizes what he states to be the main distinctions between the two traditions in terms of Table 1.

Table 1 American and European organization theory:
a comparison

	American	European
Approach	Microscopic (behavioural)	Macroscopic (structural)
Field of study	Organizational psychology	Organizational sociology
	Man-in-organization	Organization-in-society
Focus on	People: their needs and attitudes	The organization as a whole
	What goes on inside the system	What is going on between the system and its environment
Emphasis	Functional (process-oriented approach)	Structural
Methodology	Laboratory experiments, surveys, observation, longitudinal, one-case studies	Comparative case studies
Ideology	Harmony-based; status-quo (conservative)	Conflict-based
	Anti-Marxian	Marxian
Central orientation of influential writers	Practical theorists	Abstract theorists
	Associated with business schools	Associated with departments of sociology
	Having close ties with the business community	Having casualties with the business community
	Know-how or technique-oriented, e.g. Human Resources Accounting, Transactional Analysis, MBO, T-Group, Control Graph	Know-why or theory-oriented

Table 1—continued

	Intent on discovering the 'one-best way'	Intent on demolishing the 'one-best way'
Examples of approaches to:		
a job design	Job enrichment	Sociotechnical systems
	Informal participative management	Industrial democracy
b organization development	Human processual	Techno-structural

Source: Kassem (1976b)

In a loose and schematic manner it has been possible to distinguish, at least in caricature, a field which claims as its rule of functioning the discursive space of Europe, organizations and power.

Within this space, which is certainly not coherent throughout, we require some point of departure, or some compass with which to steer a course. We might be tempted to start with the concept of 'power' as our point of departure. While the notion of a distinctively European tradition of organization theory may exist only as an idealization, or even as something (a parochial discourse) that we might not wish to achieve, power itself would seem to be less problematic. It cannot only be mere caricature.

If the concept of power is 'essentially contested' (Lukes, 1974), this would seem to imply that it does have some substance. Our certainty on this score would begin to recede just as soon as we became aware that what 'essentially contested' might mean is itself open to question. The idea of 'essentially contested' concepts derives from Gallie (1955) and includes as one of its defining characteristics that a concept is essentially contested when it derives 'from an original exemplar whose authority is acknowledged by all the contestant users of the concept' (Gallie, 1955, p. 180). Lukes (1974, pp. 26–7) rejects the claim that there is in fact any one original exemplar which can be said to have once authoritatively defined 'power'. He cites Parsons' various uses of the concept of power (Parsons, 1957; 1963a; 1963b) and Arendt's (1970) as contrary exemplars to that which Dahl (1957) assumes to be 'original'. One could compound this list of contradictory usage quite easily.

This implies that 'power' is not an 'essentially contested' concept in the way Lukes has suggested, after the manner of Gallie (1955). In addition, it implies, as MacDonald (1976, p. 381) stresses, that 'if a concept is truly essentially contested, the proper ground for contest is the essence of the concept', not value judgments about the use of the concept, as Lukes (1974, p. 26) maintains. It would seem that we can accept neither that power is an essentially contested concept in Gallie's terms nor that Lukes succeeds in substituting an alternative definition of an essentially contested concept which would enable it to be seen as such. Lukes is apparently as confused and confusing as MacDonald (1976, p. 381) argues.

This is not to suggest that Gallie's original definition is in itself 'uncontestable'. One way of showing some of the problems with the idea of an uncontested original exemplar of definition would be to consider the work of a political philosopher who has attempted to argue that the 'political' (including 'power') is essentially contested, and that the essence which is contested is one which is rooted in an original usage. Wolin (1960) provides such an example. Wolin has faced issues similar to those which animate MacDonald's (1976) dispute with Lukes (1974), although he does not do so by reference to Gallie (1955). By posing the primacy of a *tradition* in the discourse of political philosophy as a unity cross-cutting time, place and substance, he presumes that 'power', as an element of the 'political', is essentially contested.

Wolin (1960, p. 3) indexes the existence of a tradition by 'a sufficiently widespread consensus about the identity of the problems to warrant the belief that a continuity of preoccupations has existed'. He identifies this 'continuity of preoccupations' with the problem of order, arguing that this problem has functioned as the locus of political discourse, particularly when crisis and disruption have occurred in the conventional political order of the time. In relation to these political 'disorders', this continuity of preoccupations is seen as essentially 'conservative':

> Of all the restraints upon the political philosopher's freedom to speculate, none has been so powerful as the tradition of political philosophy itself. In the act of philosophizing, the theorist enters into a debate the terms of which have largely been set beforehand. Many preceding philosophers have been at work collecting and systematizing the words and concepts of political discourse. In the course of time, this collection has been further refined and transmitted as a cultural legacy; these concepts have been taught and

5

> discussed; they have been pondered and frequently altered. They
> have become, in brief, an inherited body of knowledge. When they
> are handed down from one age to another, they act as conservatizing
> agencies within the theory of a particular philosopher, preserving the
> insights, experience and refinements of the past, and compelling
> those who would participate in the Western political dialogue to
> abide by certain rules and usage (Wolin, 1960, p. 22).

This idea of tradition is almost too appealing—certainly Wolin is
not the only person to have been attracted to it (see Clegg, 1975).
However, its appeal is somewhat suspect precisely on the grounds
which Gellner (1967) uses to criticize Gallie. For it presupposes 'an
historically invalid and logically irrelevant "point" of origin', as
MacDonald (1976, p. 381) puts it. In doing so it serves as a
rhetorical way of silencing doubts and questions, and of proposing
historical verities of temporality, succession, similarity, continuity
and conservation. This conservatism is most manifest in its
necessary insistence that the 'tradition' is not subject to much in the
way of radical change. Such changes as do occur are attributed to
theorists recoiling from the disorder of the world external to their
discourse.

> Just as history never exactly repeats itself, so the political experience
> of one age is never precisely the same as that of another. Hence, in
> the play between political concepts and changing political
> experience, there is bound to be a modification in the categories of
> political philosophy. . . . The result is that each important political
> philosophy has something of the unique about it as well as
> something of the traditional (Wolin, 1960, p. 25).

In this it shares with conservative and organic theories the belief
that social change should, wherever possible, be attributed to
factors exogenous to the system. Where change cannot be
assimilated to such 'realist' assumptions, then it can be adduced to
the causality of a residual category, such as 'genius':

> Whatever the truth of Whitehead's dictum that 'creativity is the
> principle of *novelty*', in the history of political theory, genius has not
> always taken the form of unprecedented originality. Sometimes, it
> has consisted of a more systematic or sharpened emphasis of an
> existing idea. In this sense, genius is imaginative recovery. At other
> times, it has taken an existing idea and severed it from the connective
> thread that makes an aggregate of ideas an organic complex. A
> connective thread or unifying principle not only integrates particular
> ideas into a general theory, but also apportions emphasis among
> them. If the unifying principle should be displaced, propositions

within the complex which theretofore were commonplace or
innocuous suddenly become radical in their implications. . . . This is
because a political theory consists of a set of concepts—such as
order, peace, justice, power, law, etc.—bound together . . . by a
fund of notational principle that assigns accents and modulations.
Any displacement or significant alteration of the notational principle
or any exaggerated emphasis on one or a few concepts results in a
different kind of theory (Wolin, 1960, pp. 24–5).

To propose a category such as 'genius' as an explanation for a
particular social theory as an artefact is to argue in terms of
'creativity' as opposed to 'production' (Zeraffa, 1976), in terms of
individual irrationality as opposed to social explicability. Such
issues dominate the sociology of literature. To pose 'production'
against 'creativity' is to locate and situate a text as a practice, as an
artefact, rather than as a creation *ex nihilo*. The writer, as a
producer, is working with theory, with fiction, in creating theory,
in creating fiction. Theorizing or fictionalizing is a method for
re-forming 'ideas, values, principles and theories which have
seemingly some explanatory meaning for society as a whole'
(Zeraffa, 1976, p. 37), for showing them in some of their many
possible ways, in those ways in which they have meaning for their
producer. Thus, essentially, the production of theory, of fiction,
becomes a way of showing possible modes of social being, as the
exemplification of the 'subjective consciousness' of a 'particular
class' as Zeraffa (ibid.) puts it.

In this sense, then, the theorizing of 'tradition' betrays a concern
with origins, influences and schools, with 'breeding' and
'pedigree', much as those feudal remnants, the aristocracy, do in
their cultivation and display of 'taste' and of 'correct form'. This
notion of tradition, with its progressive refinements, constantly
seeks to re-create the mythology of the origin, the beginning, in its
permanence as the way of classifying contemporary discourse.
Contemporary discourse can only be judged by reference to an élite
which rules because it survives; it survives through being treated as
an élite. Like great families, the origin and its traces persist through
'tradition'.

In more recent versions of the notion of 'tradition', emphasis has
shifted from continuity to revolution, from the slow and stately
progression to what Foucault (1972) has termed 'interruptions':

> *The epistemological acts and thresholds* described by Bachelard:
> they suspend the continuous accumulation of knowledge, interrupt
> its slow development, and force it to enter a new time, cut it off from

its empirical origin and its original motivations, cleanse it of its imaginary complicities: they direct historical analysis away from the search for silent beginnings, and the never-ending tracing back to the original precursors, towards the search for a new type of rationality and its various effects (Foucault, 1972, p. 4).

What this 'new type of rationality' seeks to analyse is the unity *presumed* by the closure of tradition, which immediately casts that which does not strictly belong or conform to it as inferior, as unworthy. It will make its analysis through the formulation of *rules* of production and through the disclosure of the rules of functioning of the *mode of rationality* of a practice. This practice is the relation constituted between statements which have hitherto ordinarily been taken for granted as the unity of a field, or fields, created as a *discourse* in whose unity one temporarily suspends belief. One does this in order to re-form any given field (perhaps even as it was), on the basis of a critical enquiry.

This way of proceeding might seem perverse. 'It would seem to be the proper thing to start with the real and concrete elements, with the actual pre-conditions', as Marx (1970, p. 205)[1] ironically suggested in the context of his discussion of 'the method of political economy'. If we were to take this suggestion 'seriously', *literally*, then our discourse on power in organizations would start in the sphere of organizations, from the standpoint of organization theory, with the exercise of power over decision-making by individuals in the organization system.

Closer consideration would show how and why this method was wrong. *Decision-making is an abstraction, if, for instance, one disregards the issues of which it is composed. These issues, in turn, remain empty terms if one does not know the factors on which they depend.* These factors would be such as 'wage-labour, capital, and so on'. What would be decisive would be the material interest of these factors in any concrete situation. To rephrase Marx (1970, pp. 205–6) slightly,

> If one were to take organization as the point of departure, it would be a very vague notion of a complex whole and through closer definition one would arrive analytically at increasingly simple concepts; from imaginary concrete terms one would move to more and more tenuous abstractions until one reached the most simple definitions. From there it would be necessary to make the journey again in the opposite direction until one arrived once more at the concept of organization, which is this time not a vague notion of a whole, but a totality comprising many determinations and relations.

How is one to make this journey? Not through organization theory, for, if I am not to disregard what I have proposed with David Dunkerley elsewhere (Clegg and Dunkerley, 1977), this discourse, in addition to whatever else it may do, provides an ideological gloss on our literal way of seeing the world as composed of 'real and concrete elements' such as organizations. This way of seeing then becomes the basis of an arguably false ontology. This ontology is that alluded to by Eldridge and Crombie (1974, p. 11) in their citation and discussion of the following story invented by Alasdair MacIntyre (1971, p. 260):

> There was once a man who aspired to be the author of the general theory of holes. When asked, 'What kind of hole—holes dug by children in the sand for amusement, holes dug by gardeners to plant lettuce seedlings, tank traps, holes made by roadmakers?' he would reply indignantly that he wished for a *general* theory that would explain all of these. He rejected *ab initio* the—as he saw it—pathetically common sense view that for the digging of different kinds of holes there are quite different explanations to be given: why then he would ask do we have the concept of a hole?

Eldridge and Crombie regard MacIntyre's tale as 'cautionary', and one whose message might well be addressed to organization theorists. This is because, when reviewing that which constitutes the arena of organization theory, 'one cannot help noticing the bewildering array of treatments from different disciplines which occur when organizations are actually described and analyzed' (Eldridge and Crombie, 1974, pp. 11–12). They remark that the nature of this enterprise is to develop a unifying conceptual framework

> . . . [which] may prove stultifying rather than liberating and the identification and handling of problems in the field standardised rather than innovating. The quest for scientific maturity might in fact end in stagnation. This leads us, not to doubt the usefulness of interdisciplinary work in the analysis of particular problems, but to argue that . . . a sociology of organizations has a claim to be considered in its own terms, rather than as some inferior species of activity the value of which is only to be measured in terms of its contribution to general organization theory.

A sociology of organizations is no less problematic than a generalized organization theory. It posits the ontological existence of *the organization* as neither a real object of enquiry, nor as an ideal theoretical object without a real object of analysis,[2] but as a multiplicity of such concrete pre-analytic and naive objects. It is the task of critical analysis to dissolve these. As Habermas (1973, p.

183) says, 'criticism is brought to bear on objects of experience whose pseudo-objectivity is revealed . . . [and] is characterized by its ability to make unconscious elements conscious in a way which has practical consequences. Criticism changes the determinants of false consciousness'.

Is it the case that organizations can be considered to be a *theoretical* object, or are they, conceptually, to be considered as the false-consciousness of a pseudo-objectivity?

How many kinds of organizations are there?[3] Say manufacturing, retailing, educational, government, criminal, military, voluntary, political, religious? There are *countless* kinds: countless different kinds of use of the juncture of materials with ideas about the relationship of these to each other. This multiplicity of kinds of organizations is not something fixed, given once for all; but new types of organization come into existence, and others become obsolete and get forgotten.

How *is* one to compare this multiplicity? Etzioni (1961) has suggested a classification in terms of bases of compliance and control ranging from moral to coercive, and suggests that the kind of commitment and involvement forthcoming from members of the organization will vary depending on the nature of the power means—coercive, remunerative or normative—that are mobilized. While such a classification enables us to compare a concentration camp, say, with a church, in terms of the types of power used in each to structure social action, it does not enable us to compare the differing power-structure positions of a commandant and a cleric within the two organizations. It is a descriptive rather than an explanatory schema.

Explanatory schemas do exist. What they seek to explain is the structure of the organization as a different type of theoretical object. Stogdill (1971, p. 4), for instance, lists eighteen basic premises and orientations to the organization as a theoretical object, and notes that his classification is certainly not exhaustive. He observes that 'which concepts and problems are regarded as important in the study of organizations are determined in part by the view or combination of views held by the theorist, in part by the philosophical and professional schools to which he subscribes, and in part by the individual conceptualizations he wishes to advance' (Stogdill, 1971, pp. 3–4). Katz and Kahn (1966, p. 18) have suggested that the organization as a theoretical object be regarded as corresponding to either a 'closed' or an 'open' systems model. Silverman (1970, ch. 2) has proposed that these be further sub-divided to include 'partially open systems' as well, and then suggests that, as an alternative to systems theory generally, the organization should be considered to be, in an 'action' perspective, 'the outcome of the interaction of motivated people attempting to resolve their own problems' (Silverman, 1970, p. 122).

Conscious attempts have been made to remedy this proliferation of theoretical objects in the area of the organization through the development of comparative study of organizations as real objects. Depending upon the particular basis of comparison, organizations are seen as having something in common, such as beneficiaries (Blau and Scott, 1973), degree and type of compliance involved in membership (Etzioni, 1961) or, most popularly and recently, organization structure (e.g. Pugh and Hickson, 1976).

Comparative analysis of organization structure proceeds on the basis of a 'systematic comparison of a fairly large number of organizations in order to establish relationships between their characteristics' (Blau, 1965, p. 323). In order to do this, when one is comparing qualitatively very different phenomena, one requires some measure or value which can be applied irrespective of any particular qualitative features of the organization in question. Pugh and Hickson (1976) attempt this through the comparison of organizations on five 'empirically derived' (from factor analysis of data measured by pre-test factors derived from fieldwork and from the organizations' literature) structural variables. These were specialization, standardization, formalization, centralization and configuration. This enables the researcher to compare a wide range of phenomena taken to be distributed across a wide range of organizations.

The method has one serious drawback. It seriously neglects the real differences between different types of organizations in terms of what they do, in favour of the way in which they are able to do whatever it is that they do. Hence, it becomes feasible to compare two qualitatively different types of organization—such as a university and an energy utility—and to report that they are quantitatively different in terms of their structures of decision-making. Not all theorists are happy about the loss of institutional specificity which this approach engenders. Crozier (1976, p. 195), for instance, says that it suffered 'three very strong biases':

> First, it was very deterministic in an old-fashioned, simplistic way which was not adequate for a phenomenon of high order complexity such as organizations; second, it was incapable of dealing with the cultural variables and tended to overemphasize a universalistic one

best way; third, it never questioned the implicit assumption it made
of equating structure (and practically formal structure) with all other
organizational characteristics since it made structure the only
mediating link between the environment of an organization and its
output. True enough, the theoretical view was much more complex,
but the necessity of measurement forced most authors to this
reductionist position at the operational, that is, at the crucial level.

Writers such as Hyman and Fryer (1975) have explicitly rejected
the view that any type of organization can be regarded as a real
object for the purposes of organizational analysis. They do so with
particular reference to organizations such as trade unions. This is
because of such specifically institutional features of trade unions as
their 'formal democratic character', the 'ambiguity of their goals'
and their existence as 'secondary organizations', inasmuch as the
existence of trade unions presupposes 'the existence of economic
institutions employing wage labour' (Hyman and Fryer, 1975, p.
158).

Clearly the concept of organization has a number of referents: it
can refer to bodies as diverse as a trade union and a prison, as real
objects, or to theoretical objects of a bewilderingly problematic
range, all too easily sacrificed for simplicity. Just because we
ordinarily use the term *organization* to refer to things as diverse as
a camp-site or the United Nations it does not necessarily mean that
anything we so label has some common feature, some essence,
constitutive of any and every organization. We may be mistaken,
or in danger of making a serious category error, if we use the term
indiscriminately. In short, it seems exceedingly difficult to identify
any field of reality which is 'organizations', except at the most
general level.

Having estranged the topics of my discourse—power, organizations, Europe—it now becomes imperative to begin reconstituting
the field of enquiry. But this cannot be easy. A critical enquiry into
the concept of power and its use in organizational analysis has to
make problematic not only the fields of power and organization
theory, but also any attempt to construct or to appropriate
unsecured grounds external to the discourse which it constitutes.
Sociology also has to be made problematic, and as a general
method for doing so, we can turn to chapter 2.

Chapter 2
Method and sociological discourse

The proper relationship between the geosphere of geology, or the biosphere of ecology, and its respective *logos*, has been the subject of considerable discussion in recent years—particularly with the emergence of ecology as a subject of popular speculation in the 1960s. The relationship between 'sphere' and '*logos*' has taken on a new criticality which centres on the indissolubility and irreversibility of the relationship of '*logos*' to 'sphere', which Commoner (1971, p. 33) has crystallized as the 'first law of ecology': everything is connected to everything else. In terms more familiar to sociology, one might say that all the sciences would seem to be increasingly characterized by a growing awareness of the reflexivity of their enquiries. The passivity of subjected spheres, such as nature, mankind or, in particular, womankind, can no longer be assumed. To use Derrida's (1968) phrase, it is the fallaciousness of logocentrism which enables us to think in terms of oppositions such as object/subject, viewer/viewed or *logos*/sphere.

Following Derrida (1970), one can say that *logos* is not a signifying system transcending individual *socius* as signifier and signified. It cannot exist outside language. The presence of signifier/signified will always be as one in language. Neither can stand apart from the other, despite the way that the metaphors of '*logos*' attempt to trace their difference. In ecology this difference is in terms of our relationship to the material world, rather than our dwelling-within-it, while in sociology it is in terms of our relationship to, and our dwelling-within, the material word. Signifier (*logos*) and signified (*socius*) are one within language, but are posed as oppositions within sociology. As this chapter will go on to argue, the resolution of this opposition has tended to be in terms of either the assimilation or the annihilation of either one of the constituent parts of sociology by the other.

Sociology, as a metaphor, stands as a figure of speech which implies but does not explicitly state a comparison between two objects or actions, between the signifier *logos* and the signified *socius*. To investigate the metaphor of sociology is to question what it implicitly is. It is to seek its essence between that which it is of, but which it is not. 'Essence is expressed by grammar', says Wittgenstein (1968, par. 371). Essence is not a thing but the underlying relation between any one thing and another which makes a specific something or other. So sociology is the relation between society and *logos*.

Originally *logos* meant that order which pervaded and grounded all things with intelligibility. This order represented, as *The Penguin English Dictionary* so concisely puts it, 'the Word of God incarnate'. A *socius-logos* would thus be the Word of God embodied in the words of men about the words and doings of men.

Comte's title of *sociology* for the new positive science of society preserved God at its very centre, albeit in charade. Comte's priesthood was to be the embodiment not of God's word, but the word of Reason, as it charted the positive laws of society from its ascendancy in post-Newtonian consciousness. Comte's proposed sociology was a programme for the moral regeneration and guidance of a society which, in the conservative view, required protection from critical Reason. If the French Revolution was the result of Reason, then it would reasonably seem that this faculty required restraint. Moral, conceived as traditional, authority had to be fostered in order to ensure that the restored social order be preserved from chaos. Comte's *savants* should not be taken as a grotesque misconception of the infant sociology at its christening. As a concrete version of *logos* they are implicit in the sociological metaphor.

One possible version of the subsequent history of sociology might depict it as the rationalization of the ideal of moral authority, initially formulated by Comte in the archaic idea of the *savants*, through the rationalization of method. This rationalization merely serves to reconstitute the metaphor monadically: sociology becomes a discipline whose recurrent motif would seem to be a desire for the annihilation of one or other of its constituent parts by the other. Stated prototypically, this nihilism has been most frequently expressed in the desire to submit the *socius* to the *logos*, with the reverse movement sometimes being posited as a radical departure (viz. ethnomethodology) rather than as a mirror image, a mere reflection. Another way of expressing this would be to say that one way of showing sociology—one way of formulating it—might be to inscribe it as an oscillation between epistemological authoritarianism and liberalism. This tension results from the following. Sociology presumes to produce morally authoritative words about the conversation and happenings of mankind, words whose authority, if not unquestioned, will at least be taken seriously. In this respect it is, as Comte and Saint-Simon correctly formulated it, the heir to religion. Conventionally, the Christian religion had solved its problem of authority by counterposing the priesthood between men and God.[1] Only they could interpret the sacred texts correctly and mediate between God and the mundane world. They were in this respect the rationalized bearers of the originally prophetic and charismatic message.

Sociology, as *the* social *logos* (that which aspires to One speech about the many), if it were not to perish with the sects of time, had to have its Durkheim. As a specific someone or other, Durkheim was historically necessary in order to routinize the charismatic conception of the secular *socius-logos*, through *The Rules of Sociological Method*. For, if there were no rule to sociological method, then how could its pronouncements be valued? And if its pronouncements were not valued, how could it ever produce social order?

Durkheim attempted to found sociology on reasonable ground by an act of faith and wilful stipulation. This involved redefining and replacing God in *logos*. Henceforth, *logos* was to be conceived as the rule of method. Durkheim's programme consisted precisely in its intent to subject human intelligence to 'the facts', reconceived as the moral order, as Bauman (1976) has argued. But 'the facts', like God, are not immediately accessible to the layman, who may be so easily bewitched by 'crudely formed concepts':

> Man cannot live in an environment without forming some ideas about it according to which he regulates his behaviour. But, because these ideas are nearer to us and more within our reach than the mental realities to which they correspond, we tend naturally to substitute them for the latter and to make them the very subject of our speculations. Instead of observing, describing and comparing things, we are content to focus our consciousness upon, to analyze, and to combine our ideas. Instead of a science concerned with realities, we produce no more than an ideological analysis (Durkheim, 1938, p. 14).

Ordinary conceptions of ordinary men about their ordinary environment are to be distrusted as 'dangerously incorrect', so much so that they might lead to 'art' rather than to 'science' (an argument which Schutz (1967) and ethnomethodology were to reverse at a much later date). Such dangerous notions had to be re-formed. *Socius* must submit to the *logos* if the 'idols' of

15

'everyday experience' are not 'to exercise undue ascendancy over the mind and to be substituted for the study of facts' (Durkheim, 1938, p. 17). Facts require method to be visible.

Durkheim's strictures on method may be regarded as a way of producing the social order that will be sociology. Sociology's version of the problem of order is precisely this: if men are left to their naive judgments they will fail to focus on ideas as if they were factitious, as if they were things. Instead, ideas 'as products of everyday experience' will have as 'their primary function' the task of putting 'our actions in harmony with our environment' according only to their 'useful or disadvantageous qualities'. Empirically, for Durkheim, such a self-interested relationship would be represented by the metaphor of 'egoistic suicide'.

Sociology's methodological solution to its problem of order is to consist in treating of itself through its own idea of treating all phenomena as if they were things. Treat the sociological method as a thing and 'facts most arbitrary in appearance will come to present, after more attentive observation, qualities of consistency and regularity that are symptomatic of their objectivity' (Durkheim, 1938, p. 28). *Logos* is rationalized into method as an idea and then treated as if it were a thing. As Durkheim (p. 28) advises, '*The voluntary character of a practice or an institution should never be assumed beforehand.*'

> Classically, where faith has been invested in the conception of a transcendent unitary god who is universal, the more there arises the problem of how the extraordinary power of such a god may be reconciled with the imperfection of the world that he has created and rules over (Weber, 1965, p. 138).

The distinctive problem of theodicy resides in the fundamental presupposition that 'even a meaningful world order that is impersonal and supertheistic must face the problem of the world's imperfections', as Weber (1965, p. 139) raised the issue.

In terms of sociology, and its own theoretical social order, the problem of theodicy has generated an entire epistemological debate stalked by the demons of nihilism.[2] Nihilism pertains where evaluation proceeds either by wilful stipulation, which may as easily be negated as affirmed, or through liberal-plural epistemologies. In these, a number of equally wilful stipulations coexist in a state of more or less peaceful coexistence or competitive incommensurability. Where this is the case, any one paradigm may be as valid as any other, within its own commitment.

The nihilism of wilful stipulation seeks ascetic salvation through the rationalization and purging of doctrine. The nihilism of liberal-pluralist doctrine seeks salvation through the aesthetically joyful expression of polytheism. It proposes a relativistic world of distinctively ordained deities and practices. Monadism or relativism come to be the twin poles of our contemporary epistemology. They are the demons of our sociological existence.

How does one drive the demons out? Certainly not within the terms of the demonology itself. One might instead want to insist that the problem resides within a framework in which such demons are possible, on the assumption that demons, however apparent they appear to be, will always be the result of alienated human practice. Such practice can provide no solution for the salvation of social theory from the fall from grace that it exhibits in the polymorphous complexity of its own genesis. The problem is the problem. It results from a situation where the ideal discourse is posited on an essentially nihilistic standard, so that whatever might be said or written is irredeemably valueless. This is because both monadism and relativism are locatable within the

> problem posed by the system of primitive terms (or the
> 'transcendental framework') within which we organize our
> experience *a priori* and prior to all science, and do so in such a
> manner that, of course, the formation of the scientific object
> domains is also prejudiced by this (Habermas, 1974, pp. 7–8).

This 'transcendental framework' is ontologically rooted within two distinct realms of ordinary life. These are the realms of *instrumental* and *communicative* action (Habermas, 1974, p. 8). The practical interest of the person engaged in instrumental action is in the control and manipulation of objects. In it is grounded the empirical-analytical project which slowly developed into the positive sciences. In the realm of communicative action is rooted the hermeneutic project which has culminated in the interpretive sciences, of which ethnomethodology is the most recent and positive flowering. These sciences result from the systematic objectification of these two concerns of daily life: control of objects and communication between subjects. The minutes of this process of 'systematic objectification' are to be found in any account of methodological procedures and puzzles.

The objectifications of positive science have clustered around the icon of the methodological purity of the one science. This has been premised on the ideal of the exact natural sciences as the perfect practice. This perfection would be most fully realized in causal explanation, which was capable of being replicated across comparable data.[3] The objectifications of hermeneutic science have clustered around the interpretation of meaning, in particular the problem of privileged access to the 'intentions' or 'motives' of the 'other' as causal springs of social action.

These two modes of the 'transcendental framework' each present particular types of problems in any substantive research pursued under their auspices. What might at first acquaintance appear to be problems of the field in which one operates, or of the concepts with which one is working, can on further reflection frequently be seen to be posed by the constraints of the transcendental framework. Within the general area of the concept of 'power', for example, one can immediately think of the debate between Dahl (1957) and Bachrach and Baratz (1970) as falling within this scope.

Dahl (1957) has consciously tried to develop a behavioural political science. He is located squarely within the transcendental framework of the positive sciences.[4] Epistemologically, Dahl's gambit has been to secure knowledge on the agreement of measurements which are operationally defined in overtly observable and causal terms. Such an enterprise predicates a number of problematics, some of which concern the 'internal' coherence ('reliability') of the measuring instruments, while others concern their coherence with a world of 'external' data ('validity'). While questions of internal coherence are of interest in posing the limits of ingenuity within the framework, criticism becomes socially potent when it is focused upon the terms of the 'possible society' in which the theorist predicates his formulations.[5] Criticism concerns the validity, rather than the reliability, of a body of knowledge or discourse under consideration. The reliability of a knowledge-domain is not its primary critical interest. The first stage of criticism is to move from a purely technical interest in reliability to a concern with the validity of the 'possible society' which is formulated. This entails asking to what extent does the 'possible society' enable us to assemble a theoretical object and practice which capture the diversity of that everyday life they purport to depict? This first stage of criticism involves the comparison of the theoretical object—the 'possible society'—not only with those formulated by other theories, but also with the living, and lived, history of daily life. This is the substance of Bachrach and Baratz's (1970) critique of Dahl's work.

Bachrach and Baratz elect not to live within the 'possible society' that Dahl's theory formulates because, as they argue, it only enables us to see overtly measurable power. They argue that, although this may seem a hard-headed and methodical premise from which to produce scientific work, it may none the less fail to account for decisively important 'unmeasurable elements' which are not part of the world of observable behaviour. Such 'unmeasurable elements' derive their social significance not from what is, but from *what is not*. Their significance as meaningful action is precisely that they do not issue in observable and measurable behaviour. In this way they introduce the concept of 'non-decisions' into the discussion of power. This concept is meant to index the type of situation in which power is displayed, not in the frequency with which some person's proposals are followed and the significance of these according to some theoretically internal criteria, but in the way in which these proposals do not significantly effect the interests (again decided on some internal theoretical criteria) of some agent or agency, almost as a matter of course. Proposals and action which would significantly effect these interests remain unarticulated: they are 'non-decisions'.

The crucial distinction between Bachrach and Baratz and Dahl is that Bachrach and Baratz do not simply rely on the outcome of decision-making as their guide to power. For them, it is the questioning of prevailing definitions which define a key issue as:

> One that involves a genuine challenge to the resources of power or authority of those who currently dominate the process by which policy outputs in the system are determined (Bachrach and Baratz, 1970, p. 47).

With Bachrach and Baratz the concept of interests enters the debate. It does so in the shape of articulated grievances—that is, through an awareness of *subjective* interests. But, as Lukes points out, Bachrach and Baratz still insist on observable conflict as a criterion for a non-decision, and hence remain within the terms of a *behavioural* science—one that depends on manifestations as its only source of reliable data (Lukes, 1974, pp. 18–20). Their model is 'two-dimensional' because it enables us to see that the maintenance of surface order against the expressed interests of lower participants also qualifies as a 'face' of power. This formulates the 'two dimensions' of power on observable 'decision-making' and 'non-decision-making', on observable 'action' and 'inaction'. This kind of dualistic problematic is given to the discourse by the way in which it bears the traces of classical mechanics. Bearing these traces, power will invariably be discussed in such a way that the positive interest, even where articulated against, as in Bachrach and Baratz, will shape the subsequent range of discussion. Hence, the Bachrach and Baratz debate with Dahl is an argument concerning the (behaviourally) admissible grounds and parameters of visible 'power-effects', where 'effect' will be indexed by some change of state in the subject.[6] Notwithstanding any such reservations, that Bachrach and Baratz are able to raise such criticisms of the terms of a discourse shows its recentering away from a location within a positive interest to one within a hermeneutic interest. It raises issues of understanding and interpreting behaviours not as actions assembled by the conventions of the scientific enterprise, but in terms of an understanding of the actions through their intrinsic meaning.

This recentering introduces a new interest and a concomitant problematic as the focus of enquiry. The interest is in the communicative acts and meaning of the other. The new problematic will revolve around 'action' concepts such as the 'intentions', 'reasons' or 'motives' of the other. Thus, in studies of power, once one has decided on some criterion to distinguish what class of action one will include in the exercise of power, one is obliged, within the hermeneutic interest, to decide whether or not to limit power solely to instances of 'intended action' (White, 1971a, for instance). Invariably, such discussions founder on the impossibility of direct access to what the other *really* meant, said or intended. Cognitions are private. One way around this unfortunate aspect of social life has been that proposed by Winch (1958).

Winch (1958) can be interpreted as saying that we can take our interpretation of the other's acts from what one can conventionally assume the act to mean or be, within (in Schutz's, 1967, phrase) the socially available common stock of knowledge. But this is not really very satisfactory as a way of answering the critical question raised under the hermeneutic interest. To do this would be to accede to the tyranny of public opinion polls or common usage as determinants of what things are. Just because one, or many, think a thing to be so does not make it so. A common meaning may be not so much the key to interpretation as that which locks us within itself, and outside interpretation. Again, an example from the area of enquiry into 'power' is particularly apt. It is another way of formulating Bachrach and Baratz's point about 'non-decisions' and of pointing toward the difficulty one has in resolving it within the hermeneutic interest.

Perhaps the most potent type of power is that which is rarely, if ever, exercised. There is little need for it to be so. Normal states of affairs, meanings and conventions routinely appear to be natural, as if they were without interest. What might once have been called 'legitimate authority' prevails.[7] In such instances all that the conventional attribution of meaning will do is to exhibit the dominant 'theorizing power' which conceals the relation of meaning and social interest. To believe what people tell us, or to accept it as the standard of what we judge people to mean, is to make of the *socius* a quite arbitrary *logos*. It is the replacement of an undialectical logocentrism with an undialectical sociocentrism. It is a suspension of judgment and the negation of wisdom.[8]

It might appear that the options that this theorizing poses as possibilities for sociology are bleak. Either it is obliged to embody the rule of an arbitrary *logos* (positive science) or an indiscriminate and unenlightened *socius* (hermeneutic science) as its standard of discourse, or it is obliged to cease production. The three options are equally unattractive. Rationality cannot be said to be present where one submits to arbitrary scientistic criteria as one's monitor of reality any more than where one only allows reality to be in terms of some *verstehende* grasp of what others say. And silence in the face of life is a sacrilege committed to both the living and the dead.

An alternative would be to attempt an analysis which transcended the transcendental framework within which sociological discourse has so often been constituted. We might term such an endeavour 'critical sociology', in which critique is 'the essential activity of reason' (Connerton, 1976, p. 16). This 'critique' not only involves critical, oppositional thinking, but also 'denotes reflection on the *conditions* of possible knowledge' and an attempt at a 'rational reconstruction' of these (Connerton, 1976, pp. 17, 18). We can begin to formulate this position in terms of the metaphors with which this enquiry into *sociology* began.

Perhaps we should consider sociology sociologically in terms of the order (or contradictions) which it engenders. This order is that of the dyad. Its members are the *socius* and the *logos*. I have suggested that in sociology there has been a recurrent tendency for either one to assimilate or annihilate the other. Simmel (1969) suggests that this may well be a formal property of all dyadic relationships. In a dyad the social structure

> rests immediately on the one and on the other of the two, and the secession of either would destroy the whole. . . . This dependence of the dyad upon its two individual members causes the thought of its

21

existence to be accompanied by the thought of its termination much more closely and impressively than in any other group, where every member knows that even after his retirement or death, the group can continue to exist. Both the lives of the individual and that of the sociation are somehow coloured by the imagination of their respective deaths. And 'imagination' does not refer here only to theoretical, conscious thought, but to a part or a modification of existence itself. Death stands before us, not like a fate that will strike at a certain moment but, prior to that moment, exists only as an idea or prophecy, as fear or hope, and without interfering with the reality of this life. Rather, the fact that we shall die is a quality inherent in life from the beginning. . . . Ideally, any large group can be immortal. This fact gives each of its members, no matter what may be his personal reaction to death, a very specific sociological feeling. A dyad, however depends on each of its two elements alone—in its death, though not in its life: for its life, it needs both, but for its death, only one. This fact is bound to influence the inner attitude of the individual towards the dyad, even though not always consciously nor in the same way. It makes the dyad into a group that feels itself not only of authentic sociological tragedy, but also of sentimentalism and elegiac problems (Simmel, 1969, pp. 60–1).

Simmel's solution to the instability and immanent death of dyadic sociation—of which, in my analysis, sociology would be a prime example—is to introduce the third party: 'The appearance of the third party indicates transition, conciliation, and abandonment of absolute contrast' (Simmel, 1969, p. 61). Instead of the unreflexivity which issues in death—the annihilation of either of the constitutive parts by the other—this premises the reflexivity which is possible when a subject is able to act back upon itself. This subject is, quite simply and concretely, the speaking/spoken subject. In *socius* this may be the people and practices which one researches. In *logos* this will be the practice through which one speaks—the theorizing power which, to put it somewhat oddly, but dramatically, speaks one.[9]

This can now be restated without the metaphors. Criticality and reflexivity cannot be within the 'transcendent framework'. Conventionally, substantive sociological discourse has been within it. Thus, in distinction to this discourse, critical sociology seeks its standard of truth neither in correspondence with what is (as positive science does) nor in terms of its internal coherence with what it allows to be (as hermeneutic science and relativist epistemologies must do). It neither deals with an immutable object domain nor aspires to an immutable knowledge domain. Both are capable of transformation through the dialogue which is its theoretical practice.

Such a critical sociology takes as its empirical domain all discourse, all theory, all texts, to treat each as seriously or as ridiculously as the other. It will not accept that the text, the discourse, or the theory resides in a possibility constitutable only by the reality which it reports and purports to correspond to. Nor will it accept that the text's possibility is purely a matter of convention. Instead it will commence analysis with the proposition that any text is inscribed in the relation between convention and correspondence, between discourse and interest, between appearance and reality constituted in the text.

Its critical interest is thus always primarily in rupture, interruption, discontinuity and damage to the sober conventions of discourse, both 'lay' and 'academic', wherever these can be shown to be premised on the reification of such conventions into a form of life. A 'form of life' concerns that which 'has to be accepted, the given' (Wittgenstein, 1968, p. 226). In general terms the 'form of life' need not be reified; indeed, it may be no more than a fundamental physio-biological framework which is determinate of human agency and activity, as some interpreters of Wittgenstein have suggested (e.g. Hunter, 1971). However, the determination of activity does not proceed only through nature's invariances, but can also exist as a 'given' where the determinant in question is reified as a form of life in conventional practice, as if it were natural, but where in fact it can be shown to serve a definite social interest. Thus, I have rendered the notion of a form of life in a somewhat unorthodox version as:

> 'iconic': a material thing (*or practice*) whose being is inexplicable apart from the idea (1) projected on to it. The behaviour glossed by the phrase 'form of life' indicates that it is behaviour which may be shown as the embodiment of actions oriented towards a standard or measure of activity, where activity may be taken to stand for any manifestation of beings in the world who can be constituted as theoretic actors. To be a theoretic actor is to be one who could have been held to have done otherwise (Clegg, 1975, p. 35; italics added).

What this suggests is that not only the conventions which we study but also those through which we study them may be regarded as a 'form of life', in the above sense. Each practice may exist in the grasp of a theorizing power which unreflexively formulates routine convention iconically: it may be invested with an almost mystical power such that it becomes that which we could not doubt, the ground of our being and time. As Horkheimer and Adorno (1947, p. 274; quoted in Jay, 1973) wrote: 'All reification is a forgetting.'

To attempt to go beneath the surface of things in this manner is not to engage in some vain quest for influences or origins, which one plots like tributaries and streams of the great river of language and its ripples in discourse:

> We must renounce all those themes whose function is to ensure the infinite continuity of discourse and its secret presence to itself in the interplay of a constantly recurring absence. We must be ready to receive every moment of discourse in its sudden irruption; in that punctuality in which it appears, and in that temporal dispersion that enables it to be repeated, known, forgotten, transformed, utterly erased, and hidden, far from all view, in the dust of books. Discourse must not be referred to the distant presence of the origin, but treated as and when it occurs (Foucault, 1972, p. 25).

In this treatment, one can interrogate the discourse for its rule of functioning, rather than locate its origin in the traces of some once-determinate presence in either 'reality' or 'discourse'.

The purpose of the triadic resolution is this—it enables us to constitute criticality as a formal practice because it presents us with a method for attending to all discourse (lay or 'professional') as *discourse*, as a speaking spoken to *and* with. It does not simply resign us to a position in which we are unable to make any judgments about the discourse other than those imposed on it, spoken at it, through standards external to it, such as correspondence with *logos* or coherence with *socius*.

This not only involves placing in doubt 'the sociological framework' of analysis, but also involves critically appraising the various sub-totalities of discourse within which we are accustomed to thinking. It must not be presumed that the production of discourse upon such topics as 'organizations', or 'power in organizations' would be based upon the existence of these as objects. The objectivity of objects requires that their existence as objectifications be theorized. It may be the case that it is the interplay of rules which makes possible the appearance of such factitious-seeming phenomena as those practices which prescribe the existence of such topics, rather than any absolute existence on their part. With Foucault (1972, p. 25), one will ask of these practices

> by what right they can claim a field that specifies them in space and a continuity that individualizes them in time; according to what laws

they are formed; against the background of which discursive events they stand out; and whether they are not, in their accepted and quasi-institutional individuality, ultimately the surface event of more firmly grounded unities.

These 'more firmly grounded unities' will not only be the formal features of our discourse and the possibilities that it prescribes (the sociological), but may also be more 'mythical'. Our topic may turn out to be the eruption of a much more general social fiction than we could originally have envisaged had we not suspended our commitment to the more customary conventions of discourse.

Chapter 3
Power, discourse, myth and fiction

Discourse, myth and fiction

Machiavelli and Hobbes form the most important eruption in the discourse of political philosophy in that they prepare the way for its development into political science, by re-constituting discourse away from a concern with the Good—the best type of polity and ruler—to a concern with the Actual—what types of regimes exist, and what the conditions are for their development and change, stability and order. Machiavelli established the point of departure for these developments by emphasizing the role of 'interest' in political life, but it was Hobbes who first attempted to locate the potentially anarchic and egoistic concept of interest within a *social* framework. Interest, as the self-expression of the proud subjectivity of a Cartesian Ego, is unstable and dynamic because it admits of no ruler other than itself. In such a world, the multiplicity of selves have to abide in a commonwealth, if they are not to be engaged in the perpetual conflict of clashing egos and ambitions.

Hobbes' metaphor for this latter condition is 'the state of nature', a condition which is, as Macpherson (1962) argues, not a 'natural' or 'pre-civilized' state, but that 'hypothetical' state in which 'men . . . with natures formed by living in civilized society, would necessarily find themselves if there were no common power able to overawe them all' (Macpherson, 1962, pp. 18–19). It is fear of the 'common power' of Leviathan that Hobbes prescribes as the antidote to the excessive pride which he postulates as the moving force of his hypothesized dwellers-in-the-state-of-nature.

What distinguishes man from other animals for Hobbes is the phenomenon of '*voluntary motion*; as to *go*, to *speak*, to *move* any of our limbs, in such a manner as is first fancied in our minds' (Hobbes, *Leviathan*, p. 47). These actions Hobbes calls 'endeavour', which, when it is oriented towards 'something' which causes it, is called APPETITE, or DESIRE (ibid.). While animals may also have appetites, they can only have them unreflectively, while men may endeavour to achieve their ends through specific means, or powers: 'The power *of a man* . . . is his present means, to obtain some future apparent good' (Hobbes, *Leviathan*, p. 72). Hobbes argues that power, as a means to an end, can become an end in itself, and, as such, an object of appetite or desire in, and for, itself, which will be signified by the honour in which a man is held. To have considerable power signifies high esteem and honour. This is never an end in itself but only, and always, the 'present means' to 'some future apparent good'. Power, and its associate honour, is something which is never finally pledged from others, as each person always strives to increase his own possession of it, which implies the diminution of others' esteem, relatively, as one's own rises. Hence, life in 'the state of nature' is a ceaseless struggle, a war of all against all.

The desires which relentlessly motivated Hobbesian man were always of movement either toward or away from some desired or detested object. These desires, to be satisfied, demanded motion on the part of each individual attempting to achieve his ends at the expense of any other individual also attempting to achieve his ends. Satisfaction of desire *causes* the desiderata to be brought within one's grasp or possession; thus, power, as the means of possession, is always 'causal':

> Power and Cause are the same thing. Correspondent to cause and effect, are POWER and ACT; nay, those and these are the same things (Hobbes, *English Works*, 1, X, p. 127).

Hobbes presents us with a view of power which is causal. In addition, power is regarded as the possession of individuals and is expressed metaphorically in terms of motion. This causal, atomistic concept is essentially 'mechanistic', in much the same way as Galileo's physics of inertia, in that changes in state are the result of forces acting on each other in their collision in space. For Hobbes, desires collide in a relentless striving for honour, which is the movement of power.

In this break with antiquity, Hobbes not only poses a new topic through the metaphor of the 'state of nature': he also proposes it through a new method, that of 'Science'.

Hobbes' conception of science parallels his concept of the state of nature. In conjuring up the state of nature, Hobbes first has to suspend belief in the history of civil society. In commencing scientific activity, Hobbes has first to renounce the history of political philosophy. This history was for Hobbes one of 'opinions

. . . vulgarly received, whether true or false; being for the most part false' (Hobbes, *Elements of Law*, I, xiii, 3). The science with which he will replace it is one rooted in speech practices which ground the possibility of Reason. In their failure to have developed this Reason, his predecessors are 'like children' (Hobbes, *Leviathan*, p. 45)—cases of arrested or immature development:

> By this it appears that reason is not, as sense and memory, born with us; nor gotten by experience only, as prudence is; but attained by industry; first in apt imposing of names; and secondly by getting a good and orderly method in proceeding from the elements, which are names, to assertions made by connexion of one of them to another; and so to syllogisms, which are the connexion of one assertion to another, till we come to a knowledge of all the consequences of names appertaining to the subject in hand; and that is it, men call SCIENCE. And whereas sense and memory are but knowledge of fact, which is a thing past and irrevocable; *Science* is the knowledge of consequences, and dependence of one fact upon another: by which, out of that we can presently do, we know how to do something else when we will, or the like another time; because when we see how any thing comes about, upon what causes, and by what manner; when the like causes come into our power, we see how to make it produce the like effects (Hobbes, *Leviathan*, p. 45).

As Wolin (1960, p. 250) observes, 'Hobbes gives us a strikingly modern conception of philosophy as concerned with linguistic "truth"; that is with the status of logical propositions'. Thus, before Hobbes can establish dominion in either social theory or reality, he has first to exercise power over speech:

> Seeing then that truth consisteth in the right ordering of names in our affirmations, a man that seeketh precise truth had need to remember what every name he uses stands for, and to place it accordingly, or else he will find himself entangled in words, as a bird in lime twigs, the more he struggles the more belimed. And therefore in geometry, which is the only science that it hath pleased God hitherto to bestow on mankind, men begin at settling the significations of their words; which settling of significations they call *definitions*, and place them in the beginning of their reckoning (Hobbes, *Leviathan*, p. 37).

The 'state of nature' is a metaphor not only for social reality, but also for social theory. In effect, Hobbes is saying: How can one establish order in social reality if one is unable to establish order in social theory? How, indeed, can either theory or reality be truly *social* if each exists in a situation where 'everything is permitted'?

There would be no unity of discourse, just the babble of tongues.

Geometers had created for themselves a unity of discourse through the arbitrary stipulations of definitional fictions: a series of accepted propositions about the nature of geometric phenomena such as straight lines or triangles. Power over speech by arbitrary stipulation of language is the philosophers' 'Leviathan' whereby order is established in their discourse of social theory.

It is the arbitrary and opposing definitional fictions of common people that lead to the nihilism of the 'state of nature' as Hobbes theorizes it. His solution to this was quite simple: to secularize God, 'the first author of *speech*' (Hobbes, *Leviathan*, p. 33), so as to restore order in Babel, by reconstituting the 'body politic' through '*pacts* and *covenants*' which 'resemble that *fiat*, or the *let us make man*, pronounced by God in the creation' (p. 19). Men had to renounce the blasphemy of acting as if they were gods, and instead must bow, collectively, to the will of one ruler, who alone would be able to authorize order in speech and public life, through the good tyranny of the monadic definition of *Logos*.

Both social theory and social reality are to be re-totalized from their fall from grace by virtue of sovereign power: the rule of Science and the rule of the Sovereign, legitimately acceded to by the ruled. The transformation of the state of nature, in both political and public discourse, from uncivil to civil society, indicated the supremacy of reason conceived as a social construction: on the one hand, science will rule because agreement to abide by it quells dissent, just as, on the other hand, the covenant of the ruled to be ruled by the Sovereign similarly restores order. Order is signified by totality, by wholeness, by Oneness, by the completeness of the monad of discourse.

This happy state of affairs is to be achieved through a twofold fiction. First, theorize men as if they were self-possessedly contained atoms impelled by mechanistic, causal and competing subjectivities, and, second, theorize a supremely atomistic subjectivity capable of sufficient mechanistic and causal power to be the Supreme Being. This model of man fitted a particular model of society (as well as one of non-society, the state of nature), which Macpherson (1962) has termed 'the possessive market society':

> By possessive market society I mean one in which, in contrast to a
> society based on custom and status, there is no authoritative
> allocation of work or rewards, and in which, in contrast to a society
> of independent producers who exchange only their products in the
> market, there is a market in labour as well as in products. If a single

criterion of the possessive market society is wanted it is that man's labour is a commodity, i.e. that a man's energy and skill are his own, yet are regarded not as integral parts of his personality, but as possessions, the use and disposal of which he is free to hand over to others for a price. It is to emphasize this characteristic of the fully market society that I have called it the *possessive* market society. Possessive market *society* also implies that where labour has become a market commodity, market relations so shape or permeate all social relations that it may properly be called a market society, not merely a market economy (Macpherson, 1962, p. 48).

While the model of society which Hobbes constructs clearly deals with a social reality whose traces are still all too familiar, the fictions through which he makes his connections cohere themselves bear traces of an evolution. This evolution is that transformation through which fiction emerged from myth.

Zeraffa (1976, p. 77) writes, 'A popular myth creates the cosmos in which what we call human, or natural, or supernatural, are engaged in a vast but minutely particularized game of exchange and metamorphosis. . . . It deifies the human and humanizes the divine.' The myth is an organic whole located in neither past, present nor future, but which locates, *theorizes*, the possible society and states of being of a people. As such it is an architectonic creation which articulates the domains of the world taken for granted, and orders them into a symmetry quite separate from the flux of time.

Mythical structures are ahistorical venues in which constant, cyclical and symmetrical forces are enacted. This is the case in Hobbes just as much as in Hesiod. In Hesiod the mythical ages of mankind's being (Gold, Silver, Bronze, Iron) are the scenarios for an 'eternal battle over human existence' between 'the order of justice and the disorder of excess' conducted in the vision of an omnipotent god (Zeraffa, 1976, p. 78). In Hobbes the 'eternal battle' is waged between the order of a just and sovereign commonwealth and the disorder of the state of nature, a myth whose fragments Hobbes recites at length in texts such as *Leviathan. But Hobbes' fiction promises an end to myth,* and so, while replaying it, he is also involved in destroying its *purely* mythical structure in order to make way for the supremacy of fiction. In Hobbes the mythical struggle takes fictional form. Hobbes offers fiction as an end to myth, a fiction which will become the new mythology.

Hobbes' Sovereign, the fictional ruler (of science, of civil life), serves to end the mythological oscillation between order and disorder. It does so together with the fiction of subjectivity. The existence of the latter is regarded as the cause of 'the state of nature', a state of uncivility which can be remedied only through the legitimate dominion of one supreme sovereign, *the* ruler. The ruler represents the apotheosis of Hobbes' concept of power: he *is* power.

For Hobbes the supreme power is a fiction (and the fiction a supreme power). Subsequent theorists were to retransform the fiction into a myth by abstracting it from the Hobbesian context and then attempting to reconstitute order from the state of nature—the abstracted state—by recreating mythical power in personified terms. In Hobbes, individual powers were of interest only inasmuch as they premised the state of nature which Leviathan would overcome. Power was really (fictionally) vested in the Sovereign, not men, although men were theorized as having powers—the powers of possessive individualists. But these powers were the source of disorder rather than of order.

Hobbes was not alone in proposing a concept of power embodied in the supreme subjectivity of the sovereign. In the emergent form of the novel, subjectivity was also becoming sovereign in the fiction of the I, the hero, the narrator (Lukács, 1973). Both versions of sovereign subjectivity were an attempt to confront and overcome a world in which the 'state of nature', or nihilism, had become dominant. Each attempts to remake society whole again, to achieve a re-totalization of the conflicts and contradictions of market society.

Fiction and power

Such fictions, despite their demise in contemporary literature from Joyce onwards, are only too alive and well in contemporary political theory. Its proponents from 1924[1] onwards (at least in America) have been explicitly concerned as part of their official policy to construct political theory on scientific grounds. This science of politics takes 'power' as its key concept. As Blais (1974, p. 45) puts it, 'In the study of politics, power is one of the most pervasive concepts. In fact some would argue that the study of power is the study of politics.' Or, as Lasswell and Kaplan (1950, p. xiv) put it, 'Political science, as an empirical discipline, is the study of the shaping and sharing of power.' However, considerable doubts have been expressed concerning the utility of the concept of 'power'; Minogue (1959, p. 283), for instance, is highly sceptical as to whether this vital concept, despite the light and life it possesses, is capable of much in the way of illumination:

> Power as an explanatory abstraction may be compared to a bright light shining on objects from the side: lighting up a very little of everything, but illuminating nothing completely. We see a little of the side, but the face remains obscure.

Partridge (1962, p. 107) is hardly more encouraging when he remarks that:

> One might even let fall the subversive hint that the conclusion most clearly intimated by much of the recent work is that power is a concept or phenomenon, too amorphous, sprawling or chameleon-like ever to be amenable to exact identification, to say nothing of anything that deserves to be called 'measurement'. Perhaps the sociologist and political scientists would do better to search for a set of more manageable concepts to replace it with; or perhaps it is after all indispensable, but, since this is so, we must reconcile ourselves to the thought that where we are concerned with power, we must be satisfied to live with vagueness, indeterminateness and generality.

James (1964, p. 47) seems to echo this resignation when he writes of the concept of power that 'It is a great, sloppy, gelatinous mass, pitted here and there with an agitated insight'. He believes that its popularity as a concept, despite its 'sloppy' nature, is due in large part to its 'iconic', or 'talisman'-like status:

> Its current popularity is perhaps related to the predicament of . . . the scholarly mind. . . . In a world of big, managed organizations, a world dominated by movers and shakers, men that do things but do not much reflect upon what they are doing, the traditional isolation of the academic can visit upon him a mortifying sense of uselessness. The result is a kind of magic thinking response, a sort of bookish autism, in which words that smell of contest, action and empire, words like 'decision-making', 'image-management', 'total-institution' and 'power' take on special value. As one of my friends in political science once informed me, 'Power is my field. I specialize in power.' I had the feeling a priest of the sacred Midewinin was permitting me a peek into his medicine bag (James, 1964, p. 47).

Despite these doubts, Passigli's (1973, p. 163) view that 'the study of power has traditionally been one of the central concerns of political science' remains a widespread article of faith in the utility of power as a concept (viz. Oppenheim, 1961, p. 91; Dahl, 1963, p. 6; Hickson *et al.*, 1971, p. 216; Key, 1964, p. 2; Morgenthau, 1965, pp. 4–5; Ball, 1975, pp. 211–12). There are doubters of all complexions, however. Whereas Minogue (1959) might believe in political science, but not power, Simon (1957, p. 4) argues that, until political scientists have solved the problem of how to define and measure power, then the existence of a political *science* must remain in abeyance.

Simon is quite specific about how this political *science* will be constructed: through the specification of causal relationships between individuals:

> When we say that A has power over B, we do not mean to imply that B has power over A. . . . [It is] a problem of giving operational meaning to the asymmetry of the relation between independent and dependent variable . . . identical with the general problem of defining a causal relation between two variables. That is to say, for the assertion, 'A has power over B', we can substitute the assertion, 'A's behaviour causes B's behaviour'. If we can define the causal relation, we can define . . . power (Simon, 1957, p. 5)

Dahl (1963, p. 41), March (1955, p. 437) and James (1964, p. 50) argue in exactly the same individualist and causal terms, and McFarland (1969) felt able to say that 'there is considerable agreement among political theorists that the power relation is a type of causality relation'.

The implicit model of power relations which Dahl, Simon, James, March, etc.—the 'modern' school of political science— affirm, appears to resemble classical mechanics in a manner analogous to that of Hobbes. While with Dahl, for instance, the rules for constructing his discourse are mediated through behavioural psychology, the outcome is the same in that the 'grammar' of this is concurrent with that of Hobbes' materialism. In sociological analyses of power which attempt to measure it through 'registered effects' the concept is considered to be equivalent to some operationally decided response of some other person. The concept of measurement implicit in measuring synonyms for 'movement', such as 'responses' or 'effects', indicates that this movement is the result of some causal 'force' or 'action'. The concept of power is one of purely individual manifestation. Something has to be seen to have happened for us to say that something *has* happened. It would seem that Newtonian mechanics, married to Hobbesian possessive individualism, has borne the offspring of modern political science.

The Hobbesian stress on definition as the cure for conceptual ills still persists in contemporary political science. Blais (1974), for instance, believes that the 'conceptual difficulties' in the study of power, to which Meehan (1967) and Eulau (1967) allude, arise because

> The word is associated with two schools of thought, the pluralists and the elitists, who seem to talk past each other without really understanding the other side's argument. To provide a uniform language would thus be a first step towards a clarification of the debate. We suggest that causal language should be adopted because power can be equated to causality (Blais, 1974, pp. 45–6).

Riker (1964, p. 346) also wants to use the language of causality to discuss power. He argues 'that differences in the notion of cause stand back of . . . differences in the notion of power. . . . At least two main types of notions of causality are used in social science discourse. One is a notion of marginality, the other is a notion of necessary and sufficient conditions.' It is this latter concept of cause with which Riker wishes to banish loose thinking about power and causation:

> One event causes another if and only if the terminal situation of the causing event is identical in space-time location and in movers and actors with the initial situation of the caused event (Riker, 1964, p. 346).

Riker wants to equate this particular concept of cause with power. He goes on to say that 'Power is potential cause' (p. 347). This seems to me absurd, given his definition of cause, because the latter demands, *a priori*, episodic instances of social action to have occurred. A 'potential cause', in this respect, is about as sensible as talking about a potential criminal, as if criminality, like causality, was somehow present *in* the person (like a cancer?) prior to its being recognized as having occurred. (Schutz's (1967) points about retrospective meaning would be important here.) It would be almost as if criminality or cause could be *visible* without benefit of their production in, through and by definite social relations embodied in particular laws and statutes.

Blais (1974) accepts that criticisms have been made of the view that power and causality are intimately related. However, he is not prepared to accept them. Perhaps he does not understand them. Certainly, he seems to have misunderstood Gibson (1971), for he takes him to task by proposing what I take to be the latter's expressed preference for discussing power as if it were a rebuke to Gibson! Blais argues that Gibson's (1971, p. 102) remark that 'it is simply not the case . . . that to have power to do something is the same as actually to cause it to happen' is 'based on a misconception of causality. Causal statements are of the if . . . then type; they refer not to actual occurrences, but to the independent variable's "ability" to affect the dependent variable' (Blais, 1974, p. 46). This would seem to be Gibson's position exactly, when he criticizes the identity of power with causation:

> There is surely something radically wrong with this identification. It is simply not the case in any but the most idiosyncratic use of the word 'power' that to have power to do something is the same as actually to cause it to happen. It is merely to be *able* to cause it to happen. Thus it is perfectly possible to have power without doing anything at all. The policeman on traffic duty, to use an illustration of Dahl's, has the power to direct the traffic not only when he is actually directing it, but also when there is not a vehicle in sight. Power therefore cannot be defined as causal relation (Gibson, 1971, p. 102).

Gibson does not want to reject the equation between power and causality completely. He wishes to modify it, by making statements of the attribution of power causally conditional. Such statements would be of the order of 'To say that the policeman has the power to stop the traffic is to say that *if* some traffic came along and he held up his hand it would stop' (Gibson, 1971, p. 105). Thus the concept of power would be 'dispositional' (Ryle, 1949). It would describe a certain state of being, or of affairs, 'as one such that if something were to occur, such-and-such effects would ensue' (Gibson, 1971, p. 105). Power would thus become a contextually dependent concept, and any attempt at specifying decontextualized *a priori* 'bases' (Dahl, 1957) of power would have to be abandoned. Whereas Dahlian-type theorists would argue that power is equivalent to its exercise, Gibson would instead say that power is equivalent to it being possible for one to produce certain effects given the existing conditions of oneself and one's environment: 'To seek power is to seek to get into such a state, it is not in itself to seek to do anything at all, nor is it to seek to get into a state such that one *will* do something *if* the occasioning conditions arise' (Gibson, 1971, p. 107).[2] This conception of power indissolubly associates the concept with that of 'freedom': one is powerful, or has power, to the extent that there is nothing to prevent one behaving in a certain manner. Martin (1971) is also critical of the equation of power and causation. Using Dahl's (1957) 'A' and 'B' terminology, he points out instances in which A can 'cause' B's behaviour yet cannot be said to be exercising power over him. Such an instance would be where an A shouts a warning to a B to avoid a moving vehicle which would otherwise have knocked him over. A 'causes' B not to be hit by the vehicle, but in such circumstances it would seem odd to say that he has exercised power. Martin (1971, p. 241) therefore concludes that power and causality are not interchangeable terms.

Ball's (1976) critique of the equivalence of power and causality is the most sustained and thorough. He argues that the metaphors of mechanics have become so rooted as ways of assembling the concept of power that the concept, instead of being illuminated by the metaphor, has become imprisoned in it. He illustrates this argument (derived from Black, 1965, and Hesse, 1966) with reference to Dahl's use of the metaphors of causality, in which the equation of power with cause becomes increasingly specific (e.g. compare Dahl, 1957, with Dahl, 1965).

The concept of cause which Dahl and others of his persuasion, such as Riker (1964), McFarland (1969) and Simon (1957), adhere to is highly specific. Its specificity is apparent in Dahl's (1957, p. 204) insistence that there must be 'a time lag, however small, from the actions of the actor who is said to exert power to the responses of the respondent' if it is to be said that power has been exercised. The causality is one of *antecedent events*, visible through subsequent effects.

Ball (1976, pp. 203–6) develops a second critique of the Hobbesian/Dahlian mechanistic view of power as event causality. He attacks the assumption that 'There is no "action at a distance"' (Dahl, 1957, p. 204; see also Simon, 1957, p. 7; Cartwright, 1959, p. 7; McFarland, 1969, p. 10) on the basis that such a principle restricts analysis to agents which are in 'connection' (Dahl, 1957, p. 204) or 'communication' (Simon, 1957, p. 7) with each other. Such a stipulation is the necessary and sufficient grounding of all mechanistic materialisms—be they either those of Hobbes, Locke or Hume (Ball, 1976) or those of contemporary political science (for critiques of which see Clegg, 1975; Ball, 1976).

Ball (1976) wishes to overcome the 'no action at a distance' stipulation in order to allow power to be present where no behaviourally manifest connection exists, and also to restrict power to only some of the possible multiplicity of cases in which no behaviourally manifest connection exists, but in which an implicit or tacit connection can be theorized. His solution, as with so many other persons (e.g., Russell, 1938; Wrong, 1968; White, 1971a), is the introduction of intention. He argues that

> since one cannot 'exercise' anything (for example, judgement) *un*intentionally, this means that we cannot intelligibly maintain that an agent exercises his power *un*intentionally (although he may not, to be sure, *intend* all the outcomes) (Ball, 1976, p. 211).

De Crespigny (1968, p. 195) attempts to articulate some sub-divisions within the general category of intention, by distinguishing between 'particular intentions', referring to specific actions, and 'general intentions', which refer to classes of actions. Thus, he believes that an A may intend, in a general way, that a B should act in accordance with his, A's, intentions, without specifying particular instances of action which would satisfy the 'general intention'. This already begins to locate 'intention' not *in* A, as a causal source of action, but in B's *interpretation* of A's intentions, although De Crespigny does not acknowledge this. This decisive shift is signalled more fully in the following passage:

> There is a type of situation in which one might want to say that power is being exerted in spite of the fact that B *fails* to act in conformity with A's intentions. This is where B acts in accordance with what *he believes* to be A's intentions, and as he would not otherwise act, but where his belief is a mistaken one, either because A has other intentions or because he has no relevant intentions at all (De Crespigny, 1968, p. 195).

Any act of B's in, or out, of accord with whatever A thinks, is always a result of B's interpretation of, among many things, what he considers A's intentions to be. This affects, fundamentally, our concept of intention, so that one can only agree with the stress on intention of writers such as Ball (1976) or De Crespigny (1968), if one offers some additional stipulations concerning the nature of 'intention'. The concept must not be theorized as if it were something 'owned' by the person, or as if it were some state of mind prior, or antecedent, to some action (as, for instance, when Blais (1974, p. 46) argues that 'intentions just become particular types of causes'). This stipulation has to be made on the simple grounds that we can never have any way of knowing what any other person's intentions really are other than through some 'conventional' criteria for locating them in publicly available phenomena such as specific speech or other social acts (or non-actions where our conventions might lead us to believe that an action would have been appropriate where it was not forthcoming). Thus, to propose that the exercise of power must be intentional is not to say anything about the state of mind of the power-agent(s). It is to report that the agent(s) in question may be defined by the sociologist— someone who makes a point of formulating the rules or conventions operative in a social setting—as actors who may be said to orientate their actions towards rules which all may be said to partake of in some degree (if only by breaking or flouting them).

The concept of intention, deployed in any way other than this, simply limits power studies either to purely individual relationships in which we are willing to trust people as to their expressed intentions, or to the explication of causal chains of expressed intentions linking diverse actions. It is certainly not consistent with any kind of structural concept of power to locate it in the achievement of expressed (or even intuited) intentions.

It is sufficient to cite what Friedrich (1937) and Passigli (1973) term 'the rule of anticipated reactions,' in order to show that there are serious flaws in the idea that power is the achievement of intended effects. This refers to those situations in which an agent discounts in advance the power of some other agent, adjusting his behaviour accordingly, and thus making it impossible, empirically, for the mechanistic concept of power to be applicable where the behavioural change precedes the affecting force (or, in Dahlian-behavioural versions, where the response precedes the stimulus—or anticipated stimulus). Of course, this assumes that there would anyway be some common standard of measurement through which different 'responses' could be compared. As I have argued at length elsewhere (Clegg, 1975), no such measure exists other than as an arbitrary stipulation. It is rather like, to cite a mistake which Dahl (1963, p. 46) makes and which Allison (1974, pp. 134–5) quite correctly criticizes (at least in the *specifics*), assuming that an apple is equal to an orange. It is not, and never can be, in the logic of our scientific form of life, except as it is mediated through some standards—those of mass or value, for instance. There are no socially sanctioned equivalents in the discussion of power to terms such as 'mass' or 'value'. Dahl's (1957) notions of 'scope'—the range of issues—simply will not do, because issues are context-dependent in ways in which value, as a concept, is not. Although particular values may depend on the context of the particular market, their equivalence as embodiments of 'value' does not have this dependence, but is instead dependent on particular historical socio-economic conditions.

What the theory requires, and what is lacking, is a theoretical context in which to locate issues independently of their specific occurrence, so that issues may be de-contextually discussed in their indexical particulars. But such a theory of issues could not flow from a subjectivist-mechanistic problematic in which power is situated in the particular individual relation under consideration. The latter would lead us toward the fruitless task of seeking some principle of aggregation of outcomes in these particular settings which would combine into a multi-dimensional measure. Such a task would be fruitless without some criterion of 'weight' of these outcomes—and, again, this criterion would have to be some universal, independent of scope, setting, or definition of any specific research, for it to be meaningful. The general critique of operationism in the study of power negates this possibility (see Clegg, 1975, pp. 20–5).

Ball's (1976, pp. 206–8) third critique of the causal concept of power implicitly acknowledges some of those reservations about the relation between power and intention. He argues that 'power explanations cannot be causal' in the sense required by covering-law theory, 'inasmuch as there are no general *laws* available to warrant them' (Ball, 1976, p. 206).

Dahl (1957, pp. 202–3) suggests that what I have elsewhere argued are rule-guided relationships, such as those holding between traffic policemen and motorists (see Clegg, 1975, pp. 49–51), are, in fact, stable in terms of Humean causality, in which *'events regularly precede outcomes'* (Ball, 1976, p. 207). However, as Ball observes, we may ask of any instance of Humean causality, 'What form does the licensing general "law" take?' He answers this question by specifying, in terms similar to those above, that the regularity which Dahl discusses is *'not* stable in Humean terms' (ibid.). This is because

> what we observe in this signalling-obeying relationship is not the instantiation of a universal law of human behaviour, but evidence that a *rule* is being applied and widely obeyed. Its truth being contingent upon human agents' continued acceptance of, and adherence to, a rule, this inference-license is not timeless and universal—as a genuine causal law must be—but is, rather, historically situated and may be obeyed or disobeyed, changed, rescinded, broken, over-ridden, and so on. One cannot change, break, disobey (or obey), or override laws of the kind required to license causal inferences and explanations (Ball, 1976, p. 207).

In short, choice does not enter into causal relations of a strictly

Humean type. One instance of such a relation would be a chemical reaction. An acid cannot choose whether or not to dissolve in water—it just does. It has that power such that, as Harré (1970, p. 85) puts it, 'in conditions of an appropriate kind, the X will do A, *in virtue of its intrinsic nature*'. Ball (1976, p. 207) contrasts this with the ability of a Prime Minister to recommend the dissolution of Parliament 'in conditions of an appropriate kind'. Although he has the ability to do so, in virtue of the intrinsic nature of his office, he does not always *choose* to do so. One cannot formulate laws relating Prime Ministers to the dissolution of Parliaments as one can formulate laws relating acids to their propensity to dissolve in water, not even when those laws are of a probabilistic type, because the two types of relation are not of the same order. One relation is the consequence of a universal law, while the other is licensed by conventional rules. While both may serve as explanations, the latter cannot be predictively causal. Our agent(s) may choose to act otherwise than our previous observations and formulations of the rules might suggest, in a way which could never be open to an acid. (However, we may be right some of the time, and can certainly proffer plausible *post hoc* accounts of such dissolutions as do occur.)

This logical connection between 'power' and 'rules' is in fact a feature of political discourse which goes much further back historically than the mechanistic imagery of Hobbes, Locke, or Hume. This is not to suggest some original, untarnished concept of power to which we must return for enlightenment. It is simply to propose that there is more to power than its contemporary grammar would suggest. Or, rather, that one way of transcending its contemporary grammar is to review it in another historically legitimate way.

Walter (1964), in his enquiry into the Greek origin of the concept of power, observes that 'a root contained in several words associated with political power has two meanings. The verb *archein* means both "to rule" and "to start"; the noun *arché* means both "sovereignty" and "beginning"' (Walter, 1964, p. 350). He quotes from Myres' (1927) analysis of Greek political ideas that

> It is now clear that in compounds the prefix arché (as in our words 'architect' and 'archbishop') describes not merely the first or chief man of a company or organization, but the initiatory function of him who 'starts' the others to work, and originates the design which they are to complete. And this appeal to Greek practical life confirms the view that what is essential in the notion of *arché* is just

this initiatory 'push' or 'drive' with which the gifted man imposes his will and pleasure on the rest (Myres, 1927, p. 158).

This excursus suggests the following: that 'governance' and 'rule', together with the *exercise* of power, share a grammar not only of causation but also of initiative, as in Aristotle's definition, in the *Metaphysics*, of power as the beginning of a change or movement. This differs from the post-Hobbesian stress, in locating power not only in the movement itself, or in its 'effects', but in the *beginning* of any such movement or change. It locates cause in an alternative terminology to that which has been in widespread use since Hobbes.

In this alternative terminology, the limitation of power to either causation generally, or 'intended' causation in particular, would not be legitimate. One of the few contemporary writers to have adopted such a terminology, as Walter (1964) observes, is Oppenheim. Oppenheim (1961, p. 100) does not relate 'power' to the causal exercise of some facility, but to a conception of power as an adjunct of 'being' rather than 'doing'. His definition of power is 'to be able to subject others to one's control or to limit their freedom' (ibid.).

This definition begins to link power not only to 'cause', but also to 'possibility' and 'freedom'. This linkage is achieved through conceiving of 'power' as a sign which also signifies a number of ancillary concepts, such as 'control'. Control either consists in the determination of choice or operates through the management of possibilities in such a way that no choice is available. The determination of choice proceeds through either 'influence' or 'deterrence'. These are still constituted as causal relationships whereby an A persuades a B to do, or not do, some action. However, in addition to this causal concept of control, Oppenheim introduces a further way of relating 'power' to the concepts of 'freedom' and 'possibility' implied in the notion of 'choice'. This is the category of 'having control'. It is a form of potential action, which also includes (as a corollary to 'exercising control') 'having influence' and 'having deterrence'—or, more grammatically, being able to prevent. To have influence means that an A would (be able to) dissuade, deter or otherwise influence a B from doing some intended act. To be able to prevent a B doing something means (an A's) making it impossible for the B to engage in something which he might otherwise have done. This would be accomplished by closing alternatives of action in advance of any action by the B.

It is this latter concept of 'control' which comes closest to a more structural conception of power. It complements Gibson's (1971) idea of power as a state in which there are no obstacles in the way of achieving any given desideratum. It does so by formulating the obverse state as also being one of power. Power is thus not only the liberty of the person to achieve some desideratum, but also the extent to which he is able to have and enjoy this liberty through the unfreedom of others, an unfreedom which the powerful person places in the way of the less powerful. (We shall return to this concept of control in chapter 7.)

Using the distinction between 'having power' and 'exercising power', Wrong (1968) argues that power may be regarded as both a *dispositional* and an *episodic* concept. He suggests that the dispositional, capacity concept of power necessarily implies the distinction between 'potential' and 'actual' power. 'Potential' power may be of two sorts: the potential for power (to be exercised), which he calls 'possible' power, and power as potential (to exercise), which he terms 'latent' power. A similar line is followed by White (1971b), who suggests that 'power does not exist independently of being had or exercised: that is, there is no such thing as power *simpliciter*. To suppose that it must exist to be exercised or to be had involves the mistaken proposition that the components of relationships and composites must be separable' (White, 1971b, p. 482). However, White wishes to conceptualize the exercise of power as theoretically prior to the having of power, because this latter concept—what Oppenheim initially termed control—'is best analysed in terms of some kind of capacity or ability to exercise power' (p. 483), which he goes on to define in terms of 'significant affecting'. The 'affecting must . . . be significant either for whoever achieves it, or whoever is affected' (p. 488).

This will not do. It is not at all unproblematic to argue criteria of 'significance' in subjectivist terms, whether they are those of power wielders or power subjects. This is because the beliefs which subjects hold are not themselves independent of power: it may well be that these are frequently the result of definitions of reality and possibility which, if not the direct product of power (in Marx's terms 'ideology' or 'false consciousness'), are certainly mediated through extant power processes of 'structuration' (Giddens, 1976, p. 120). While one might not want to dispute that the exercise of power concerns significant affecting, the subjectivist basis of significance that White (1971b) advances must be disputed. One might instead argue for an *explicitly theoretical* (rather than *implicitly theoretical*, as in ordinary usage) criterion of significance related to the institutional features of the setting under review. Crozier (1973, p. 214) makes this point also, when he writes that

> from a structural point of view, no power relationship can be dissociated from the institutional system or systems within which it develops. There can be no neutral field. Each power relationship is shaped by a whole series of 'structural' constraints that condition the rules of the game, and it therefore expresses, at a secondary level, the logic of the institutions or structures.

Crozier's (1973, pp. 215–16) concept of power in an institutional perspective is of 'a process developing over time that, with its goals and its rules of play, affects the organization or system within which the various parties act (or which they have formed for the purpose)'.

Such an 'institutional' perspective is hardly likely to emerge so long as theorists such as White (1971b) appear to concur with Partridge (1962, p. 110) that two-person interpersonal relationships are

> fundamental, that is they are the very relations which we find most bewilderingly and intricately intertwined, within the complex institutionalized relationships of great groups and highly organized communities . . . we cannot understand or judge the more complex structures unless we can identify the simpler forms of relations that are involved therein and determine some of their relevant qualitative features.

The implication of strictly following this perspective would be to regard power relations between America and Russia as reducible to the interpersonal relationships of the Presidents of each country. Partridge's concept of this interpersonal relationship is extremely broad: it ranges from 'influence' to 'domination', from the effect, intended or unintended, that a painter like Cézanne may exert over a generation of painters, to the situation in which 'A directs or controls the behaviour of B and where A's wishes prevail over those of B: B acts as he does only because he is compelled so to act by A, and would not do so but for A's ability to make him act in ways that he does not want to act' (Partridge, 1964, p. 111). Partridge acknowledges that 'interaction' and 'domination' may, in fact, be mutually related. A Svengali-Cézanne perhaps?

Partridge goes some way to meeting the objections which I have made to White's (1971b) criterion of 'significance'. He wishes to use the concept of power as the 'present power to produce effects in the future' (Partridge, 1964, p. 116) with reference to a 'field' of power in terms of its 'range', 'zone of acceptance' and 'intensity'. The concept of 'range' applies to 'the number of men he [the, supposedly male, power-wielder] can influence or coerce' (Partridge, 1964, p. 118); the concept of 'zone of acceptance' (Simon, 1957) refers to 'the particular set of B's interests, desires or activities that are amenable to A's influence or control' (Partridge, 1964, p. 118), while the concept of 'intensity' refers to 'the extent that another can influence or control this segment' (ibid.).

I would not wish to dispute the importance of being able to discuss power rationally—as applying to specific instances of social action, as against some other instances or all instances—but would wish to dispute that concepts such as 'range', as Partridge defines it, are appropriate means for doing so. The idea that one's power increases, invariably, with the number of men (people) that one can influence or coerce, is to take a peculiarly liberal-pluralist view of the world, in which the topic of power is regarded in personal terms as an effect of individual actions entered into by persons in an autonomous political sphere. In this perspective one can preserve the fiction of 'one person, one value', only by failing to recognize that the person's 'value' is not something determined equivalently to that of all other persons, *prior* to any exercise of power, but is in fact an unequally distributed feature of social scenes which structurally predisposes the nature and outcome of power exercises. Emmet (1953, p. 4) makes a similar observation about Russell's (1938) concept of power as the production of intended effects, in which he relates power to the greater number of intended effects that the powerful person can produce. She wonders:

> But is it useful to measure power by the *number* of achieved effects unless we take into consideration the *kind* of effect? A may have wanted to do a lot of little things, and have succeeded in doing them all. B, after a life of frustration, may have at last succeeded in one big thing. Are we to say that A has more power than B?

The traditional role of political philosophy as an adjunct to 'statecraft' and 'governance' is probably responsible for the frequency with which liberal values or ideology have been such a constitutive feature of enquiry into power. Liberalism is a theory of politics constructed out of materials whose ontological base is the individual, his/her acts, motives, intentions, etc. All other entities in the discourse of liberalism ultimately come down to the individual person. When we are dealing with issues of power, however, although our ultimate referents may be individuals, these constructions are not adequate for dealing with those aspects of power which are structurally determined, not *by* ontologically complete individuals, but *through* actual individuals in their constitution as such and such a type of person, engaged in the routine acts appropriate to their office and station. Hence, the fact that the British economy sterling balance can be affected, positively or negatively, by the utterances of prominent trade unionists, does not show that such unionists 'control' or 'have power over' the economy. Rather it implies that they are socially treated by agents and agencies *as if* they did have that power. What this serves to demonstrate is that specific types of social formation may be determinantly structured in such a way that the liberal conception of the individual's power may serve certain functions which can only obscure the structural sources of these visible effects. These structural sources may well be material practices which, because they are not visible within that sphere of life designated as the political, cannot have the same political visibility as the performances of actors constituted within this sphere. So, a trade union leader, Jack Jones for instance, may appear to be the most powerful person in Britain because his performance is treated as *the* occasion for structural agencies to articulate their effects within the economy. But this is only an appearance. It is the occasion, not the initiating instance. This is because Jack Jones is only treated as such a type of powerful person within a structural framework which allows his treatment as such to be signalled by a fall in the exchange rate, or sterling balances, and which can thus identify these actions as a symbol of the power of the person's performance.

The whole ritual maintains an illusion of individual power. This illusion serves to mask actual structures of power which are not signalled in their effects, but whose effects become merely a further occasion for reasserting the hegemony of the ideological framework which enables and justifies these structures.

The individualistic and subjectivist concept of power cannot aid us in this kind of analysis. It merely disposes us to treat illusion as reality.

Chapter 4
Power, dimensions and dialectics

Meta-theories of power debate

Contemporary theorists of power, particularly in their empirical enquiries into local communities, have conducted a protracted debate in recent years concerning the nature of power structures in these settings. Two alternative and competing views of power have been advanced. On the one hand, those whom Polsby (1963, pp. 8–11) terms 'stratification' theorists argue that political life in these communities is correctly described as being one in which governance proceeds through a relatively coherent 'élite'. On the other hand, there are 'pluralist' theorists who are more likely to maintain that power resides not in any élite, but is widely dispersed amongst many competing and countervailing groups. These groups are located with respect to widely disparate issues and have different members, resources, skills, interests and domains.

Sociologists, with their interest in issues of class, tend to be 'élite' or 'stratificationist' theorists, while political scientists tend to be 'pluralists', a distinction which Walton (1966) makes contingent upon the differing methodologies that each brings to empirical enquiry. Sociologists have favoured a 'reputational' model. This was first used by Hunter (1953). It consists of asking persons designated as 'judges', because they are 'well informed' on some criteria, to compile a list of the most 'influential' people in the community. Those whose names occur with the highest frequency are considered to be the most powerful people. Political scientists, observes Walton (1966), have tended to favour a different methodology, that of studying 'key' decisions on some criteria in a number of preselected issue areas. Those people who are observed to successfully initiate or oppose key decisions are then regarded as the most powerful members of the community. Walton wishes to relate the different findings, on meta-scientific grounds, not to an empirical disagreement about reality *per se*, but to the differing methodologies used by political-scientist 'pluralists' and socio-logical 'élitists'.

Another version of a 'meta-scientific' argument is that advanced by Ball (1976, p. 196) in connection with his critique of causality. He argues that the Community Power Debate 'controversy is rooted in two competing claims whose conceptual differences remain unrecognized. These claims are that (1) only *events* can count as causes, and contrariwise that (2) non "events" . . . may also figure as causes' (pp. 196–7). Ball's argument, like that of Lukes (1974, p. 9), is that the proper level of the Community Power Debate is at the level of *concepts*, rather than that of concrete empirical disputes, which would appear to be the grounding of most of the participants' self-understanding.

As Ball notes, the controversy rages around 'Who governs?' (Dahl, 1961), a question variously answered as either a plurality or an élite concentration of people. Ball (1976, p. 198) argues that the debate is one of unresolved conceptual confusion concerning two different and implicit conceptions of causality. Lukes (1974, p. 26) argues that there is an underlying primitive causal notion of power, but that it needs 'something further' attached to it, which is the notion that A's affecting of B should be 'non-trivial' or 'significant'.

I will reject Lukes' proposed concept of power as underlaid by a primitive causal concept. I will accept that the concept of power needs a criterion of 'significance' attached to it, but I will argue that this significance must attach to *issues*. I do not accept Ball's (1976) argument concerning two types of causality, nor do I consider this to be the underlying ground of the Community Power Debate. I will attempt to formulate the Community Power Debate as a mode of rationality within a specific form of theorizing taken as the structure within which the individualist and causal concept of power has been deployed.

Taken together, I will argue that these, in the absence of *Leviathan*, would necessarily produce the solution to the problem of order which is the Community Power Debate. Whereas Lukes (1974) argues that this debate indicates the existence of different dimensions of the same concept, I will suggest that it indicates the existence of two equally undialectical constitutions of the concept. Here I will draw on the ground laid in chapter 2. Like Lukes, I will constitute the debate as 'layered', but will not treat these layers as dimensions of the one concept, but as dialectically conceived moments in the structural production and re-production of power in social life. In so doing, I will eventually argue that the conventional concept of power is, in many ways, a surface aspect

47

of the totality of the topic of power.

The concept of power, conventionally conceived, leads quite naturally to a concern with *who* governs, and I will go on to argue that it is precisely this concern with *who*, rather than with the reflexive, theoretical and everyday production of the 'who', which intrinsically flaws conceptual solutions such as those of Lukes (1974), as well as giving rise to such debates as that which he attempts to synthesize.

For the remainder of this chapter, I will consider Ball's (1976) and Lukes' (1974) formulations of the Community Power Debate. In addition, I will reconsider my own earlier formulation of it (Clegg, 1975) in the light of the work done in chapters 1 and 2. I will not concern myself overmuch with retelling the debate itself—it would be dreary and of little immediate use here.

A mistake about causality?

Terence Ball (1976) attempts to generate an explanation of the existence of the Community Power Debate in non-empirical terms. He does so by arguing that it is a function of the use of two different concepts of causality (although he does not explain why these two views should have developed as they have). On the one hand, the pluralists have viewed only 'events' as causes, while, on the other hand, élitists have regarded 'reasons' as causes. He commences his explanation by succinctly formulating the objections of 'non-decision theorists' to that stress on overt decision-making which is characteristic of writers such as Dahl:

> Non-decision theorists hold that some would-be issues never come to light because some person or group may *believe, perceive* or *feel* that he or they could not prevail against some other group believed to be capable of blocking any such power attempt. . . . R is less likely to raise an issue if he believes that C can and probably will block his attempt and defeat it, can take reprisals against R, and so on (Ball, 1976, pp. 198–9).

Ball identifies as Friedrich's (1937) 'rule of anticipated reactions' the concept of power stated by Bachrach and Baratz (1962, p. 949) which reads:

> to the extent that a person or group—consciously or unconsciously—creates or reinforces barriers to the public airing of policy conflicts, that person or group has *power*.

Bachrach and Baratz relate the existence of these barriers to the observable actions of persons engaged in power struggles. In particular they stress the role of those over whom power is exercised, by linking them (Dahl's B's) to 'issues':

> The distinction between important and unimportant issues, we
> believe, cannot be made intelligently in the absence of an analysis of
> the 'mobilization of bias' in the community; of the dominant values
> and the political myths, rituals, and institutions which tend to favor
> the vested interests of one or more groups, relative to others. Armed
> with this knowledge, one could conclude that any challenge to the
> predominant values or to the established 'rules of the game' would
> constitute an 'important' issue; all else, unimportant (Bachrach and
> Baratz, 1962, p. 950).

For Bachrach and Baratz, non-decisions are of two types. There are those decisions that do not occur because of the less-powerful party's perception of a situation as one in which it would have been injudicious, on whatever criteria, to have raised the issue. There are also those situations where non-decisions and non-issues become defined, rather than remaining seemingly implicit, through 'challenges' to power, which, even if injudicious and ineffective, are at least aired. Thus are non-decisions given empirical shape.

There is a confusion in Bachrach and Baratz's work here, which is reflected in the different ways in which Lukes and Ball understand it. Lukes (1974, p. 19) takes the last quotation to indicate that non-decision-making must still require observable conflict for it to be seen to be present, and he quotes them to the effect that where 'there is no conflict, overt or covert, the presumption must be that there is consensus on the prevailing allocation of values, in which case non-decision making is impossible' (Bachrach and Baratz, 1970, p. 4; cited in Lukes, 1974, p. 19). Ball (1976, pp. 198–9) interprets them to the contrary. He cites a passage from quite early in 'The two faces of power' (Bachrach and Baratz, 1962, p. 949) which discusses the situation of a discontented professor, whose discontent arises from his grievance about a faculty policy of long standing. This 'professor resolves in the privacy of his office to launch an attack upon the policy at the next faculty meeting'. But he does not, and one of three reasons for his doing nothing which Bachrach and Baratz (ibid.) suggest is the 'beliefs and attitudes of his colleagues' (Ball italicizes 'beliefs' and 'attitudes' in his citation).

Ball (p. 199) interprets Bachrach and Baratz on this as implying that power does not have to be accompanied by conflict (which is contrary to how Lukes (1974, p. 19) interprets them). Ball states this explicitly in terms of 'non-events':

> Now the important thing to note here is that the professor's *belief* (about the probable failure of any challenge to 'the powers that be') is assuredly not an 'event'. Nor are the prejudices, biases, beliefs and attitudes of his colleagues 'events'. That is not, of course, to say that as non-'events' they are unreal or non-existent. They rather more closely resemble standing conditions. As such, there would appear to be no reason why beliefs (etc.) could not figure as causes of (or reasons for) certain behaviours, for example, sitting in frozen silence (Ball, 1976, pp. 199–200).

This interpretation of Bachrach and Baratz by Ball raises the issue of whether or not reasons can be causes. If reasons can be causes, then it would be sensible to say that 'beliefs', as reasons for not acting, are causal of the resultant non-action. If, however, it is not sensible to speak of reasons as causes, then the account which Ball presents of Bachrach and Baratz will itself be nonsensical. This is not an insignificant issue. It bears most directly upon whether or not power is intentional, as Kenny (1975, p. 98) suggests when he writes that 'The description of action to be done which is the conclusion of practical reasoning furnishes a description under which the action, if performed, is intentional'. In addition, if reasons are regarded as causes, then it is quite easy to see how sociocentrism would appear to be a viable alternative strategy to logocentrism. Rather than look for external, natural, social-factual causes independent of ordinary consciousness, one could look to ordinary consciousness as itself a causal agent in the production of action.

For a causal argument, such as that which Ball presents in his interpretation of Bachrach and Baratz, to be admissible as such, then two necessary features must be present in the structure of the argument. These are that the cause and the effect be both 'distinct and separately identifiable social phenomena' and that they be in a uniformly conjoined relationship (MacIntyre, 1962, p. 49). In Ball's case, this demands that 'belief' and 'action', as cause and effect, be separate and necessarily related factors.

Within ordinary usage belief and action cannot be constituted as separate and necessarily related factors, as Humean causality would require. I will argue that this is because both belief and action, as properties of being human, are constituted in and through discourse as neither necessarily separate nor necessarily related phenomena. In ordinary usage only human agents—those in possession of a language—can act. This is because, as Pitkin (1972, p. 159) puts it, 'the idea of action is essentially linked to that of an agent. For every action, there must be an agent *whose* action it is'.

Now it might seem possible that one's dog could act, could be an agent. For instance, my dog may be frequently observed eagerly anticipating (thinking?) the appearance of his close family friends at the door, prior to their actual appearance, but subsequent to the sound of a car. Dazzle (for that is my dog's name) appears to be able to discriminate between 'familiar' and 'known' car-engine sounds and 'strange' ones. His 'predictions' of the appearance of 'friends', as against 'strangers', are almost invariably correct, and always correct if the friend is myself. It would appear as if Dazzle thinks to himself something like 'That sounds like Stewart's car, therefore Stewart can be expected at any minute. This is exciting. I am excited.'

Kenny (1975) stresses that it would only *appear* to be so. He maintains that 'unless a dog masters a language it is hard to see how he can *think that he is thinking that* his master is at the door. There is nothing the dog could do that could express the difference between the two thoughts: "My master is at the door" and "I am thinking that my master is at the door"' (Kenny, 1975, p. 5).

An agent is thus taken to be the generative and reflexive source of an action, and as such may be said to *cause* the action. Thus, although my dog may not think that he is thinking that I am at the door, a person can, and her belief in my being at the door is causal of her action in opening the door to me in anticipation of my being there. Her belief in my presence is causal of her action in opening the door, or so it would seem. What does her, or any, action entail? Chisholm (1966, p. 29) suggests that action is purposeful and intentional, or, as Schutz (1967) says, it is done 'in order to' achieve some end, or 'because of' some reason. That an action can be reasoned suggests that it can be thought of as a class of 'conventional' or 'rule-guided' activity—it is something which can be done correctly or incorrectly, successfully or unsuccessfully, according to some conventional and socially located criterion of performance. Thus, power would appear to be a specific class of action exerted in the pursuit of some end which is successfully achieved, 'despite resistance' as Weber (1968, p. 53) says. If this is the case, would it be incorrect to say that the cause of an action which is an exercise of power would be the agent's belief about the worth and probability of its success? And to add that these beliefs will contain some estimate of the other's power to prevent the success of any such intended action? Can such beliefs, intentions, reasons, be causes? Is it, then, that power must be an intentional act—that one must intend some consequences of one's action, and that one's beliefs about others' propensity to oppose one's intended acts are a power phenomenon?

This series of questions clarifies a point of Ball's (1976) interpretation of Bachrach and Baratz (1962). The latter suggest that the professor's inaction is a result of his colleagues' beliefs and attitudes, while Ball maintains that it is a result of *'the professor's* belief'. Correctly one might say that it would appear to be a result of the professor's beliefs *about* his colleagues' beliefs. While the professor's beliefs may be causal of his inaction, they themselves are caused by (his beliefs about) the beliefs of his colleagues.

We have here an abundance of beliefs. Unless we can somehow separate one belief (let us call it X) from another belief (which we may call Y), then we are unable to speak of separate phenomena, and hence unable to speak of X causing Y, if X and Y are the same thing.

Our only access to knowledge of the other's beliefs would be what the other said. The criterion of causality, and thus of the presence of power, would be the other's articulated beliefs about his or her beliefs about others' beliefs! We could have no check on the truthfulness or correctness of these beliefs independently of what the other says (or said—we might use a 'consistency rule' (Sacks, 1972)). This would then be a decisive display of our commitment to a *sociocentric* epistemology, one which would be wholly uncritical—we simply would have to take the other's accounts for granted. If we did not, then we could not proceed to discuss power, intention, belief and cause as we have elected to do. In a sense we can be said to be committing our scientific knowledge about power to the private language of beliefs about beliefs that the other operates with. We could never tell whether or not any publicly available belief-utterance was a correct one—the criterion of correctness would belong to the other's private beliefs, and as such could be intelligible only to this one other person. It would be rather like the case in which Wittgenstein (1968) demonstrates that there can be no rules for correctness within a private language:

> Let us imagine the following case. I want to keep a diary about the
> recurrence of a certain sensation. To this end I associate it with the

sign 'S' and write this sign in a calendar for every day on which I
have the sensation.—I will remark first of all that a definition of a
sign cannot be formulated.—But still I can give myself a kind of
ostensive definition.—How? Can I point to the sensation? Not in the
ordinary sense. But I speak, or write the sign down, and at the same
time I concentrate my attention on the sensation—and so, as it were,
point to it inwardly.—But what is this ceremony for? for that is all
it seems to be! A definition surely serves to establish the meaning of
a sign.—Well, that is done precisely by the concentration of my
attention; for in this way I impress on myself the connexion between
the sign and the sensation.—But 'I impress it on myself' can only
mean: this process brings it about that I remember the connexion
right in the future. But in the present case I have no criterion of
correctness. One would like to say: whatever is going to seem right to
me is right. And that only means that here we can't talk about
'right'. Are the rules of the private language *impressions* of
rules?—The balance on which impressions are weighed is not the
impression of a balance (Wittgenstein, 1968, paras 258, 259).

Wittgenstein is here arguing that the ascription of meaning to a
sign is something that must be independently and publicly justified
apart from the subject's own claims to have so justified the matter.
Ayer (1966, pp. 256 ff.) objects that this makes any test of
correctness impossible, because one would never be able to
recognize anything except by trusting it to be *that* thing through
one's senses. McHugh (1971, pp. 330–1) correctly opposes this by
pointing out that such trust is not private—a feature of one's
senses—but is in fact social and public, and thus a feature of
institutional conventions. And the belief, held in common with
others in accordance with some canon or collective of rules, that a
thing is so, is quite different from a belief of one's self about one's
own beliefs which can of necessity only be known by oneself.

If these grounds are not sufficient (which I think they are) for
rejecting Ball's (1976) argument that private beliefs can be
considered to be causes, then MacIntyre's (1962) 'A mistake about
causality in social science' may suffice.

MacIntyre (1962, p. 50) proposes that the classical Humean view
of causality involved at least the following:

For something to be the cause of something else, the two must be
observed to be uniformly conjoined. If A constantly precedes B, and
B uniformly follows A, then A is the cause of B. It follows that there
is no necessity in causal relations. A is the cause of B, but equally B
might have been the cause of A, or C the cause of either or both of
them. All causal connexion is contingent and we can only discover

what causal connexions do in fact hold by looking. We ought never
to be surprised, on Hume's view, by what we discover, for we have
no right to any prior expectations which might be overthrown.
Anything may turn out to be causally connected with anything else.
From this the following paradoxical conclusion follows for the social
theorist, at least if he holds, as classical sociology has done, that
beliefs and actions are distinct phenomena.

If beliefs stand in a causal relationship (as that is understood by
Hume) then it is purely contingent which beliefs are related to which
actions. If we are looking for the cause of some action in the realm
of beliefs, we can have no *a priori* expectations about where to look.
Any belief might be the cause of any action.

MacIntyre proceeds to argue that, in fact, while 'beliefs can
sometimes be considered apart from actions', actions can never be
considered apart from beliefs: the doing of an action is a way of
showing belief in the performance. Spraying the greenfly on roses is
a way of showing the beliefs one has about the harm that greenfly
do to roses and the causal efficacy of spraying as a prophylactic
activity. MacIntyre (1962, p. 52) regards actions that belie beliefs as
'inconsistent'—someone who believes greenfly are harmful and is
concerned about the welfare of his roses, but does not spray them,
would thus be considered inconsistent. However, it could be that he
simply holds a counter-belief—that DDT is a 'bad thing', for
instance, and he will have none of it in his garden. Now we are
dealing with belief-action 'causal' relations as consistent only
within 'what the users of that language find it natural to *do*'
(Petrie, 1971, p. 147; also see Clegg, 1975, pp. 30–42). The
relationship between belief and action becomes conceptual rather
than causal. The concept of causal power allied to intentional
instances of its exercise becomes untenable in strictly causal terms.
We may conceive of such relationships conceptually, but ought not
to expect such conceptual coincidence to point to constant causal
conjuncture. What relationship there is, is one of an agent's choice,
within what he or she finds *natural* to do in constituting the
coincidence.

Dimensions of power

Let us return to Bachrach and Baratz, and Lukes' alternative (1974)
interpretation of them. Lukes (1974, p. 18, quoting Bachrach and
Baratz, 1970) maintains that

The central thrust of Bachrach and Baratz's critique of the pluralists' one-dimensional view of power is, up to a point, *anti-behavioural*: that is, they claim that it 'unduly emphasises the importance of initiating, deciding, and vetoing' and, as a result, takes 'no account of the fact that power may be, and often is, exercised by confining the scope of decision-making to relatively "safe" issues' (p.6). On the other hand, they do insist (at least in their book—in response to critics who maintained that if B fails to act because he anticipates A's reaction, nothing has occurred and one has a 'non-event', incapable of empirical verification) that their so-called non-decisions which confine the scope of decision-making are themselves (observable) *decisions*. These, however, may not be overt or specific to a given issue or even consciously taken to exclude potential challengers of whom the status quo defenders may well be unaware. Such unawareness 'does not mean, however, that the dominant group will refrain from making non-decisions that protect or promote their dominance. Simply supporting the established political process tends to have this effect' (p. 50).

Lukes argues that Bachrach and Baratz generate the Community Power Debate through 'redefining the boundaries of what is to count as a political issue by identifying *"potential issues"* which non-decision-making prevents from being actual' (Lukes, 1974, p. 19). However, unlike Ball (1976), he does not regard this as an epistemological difference because he still interprets them as 'behaviourist', albeit of a more liberal disposition than Dahl. Their behaviourism is evidenced for Lukes by their 'stress on actual, observable *conflict*, overt or covert' (Lukes, 1974, p. 19), but it does have the advantage of introducing a notion of 'interests' which is wider than that of Dahl's, with its focus purely on the realm of those policy preferences which are revealed by political participation. Bachrach and Baratz's concept of 'interests' remains 'subjective'—the covert or overt expression of grievances by individuals either within or without the political system.

Lukes (1974, pp. 21–4) regards Bachrach and Baratz's 'two-dimensional' view of power as an advance over Dahl. However, he rejects it as inadequate on three counts. The first of these is their qualified behaviourism:

> In trying to assimilate all cases of exclusion of potential issues from the political agenda to the paradigm of a decision, it gives a misleading picture of the ways in which individuals and, above all, groups and institutions succeed in excluding potential issues from the political process. Decisions are choices consciously and intentionally made by individuals between alternatives, whereas the

bias of the system can be mobilized, recreated and reinforced in ways that are neither consciously chosen nor the intended result of particular individuals' choices (Lukes, 1974, p. 21).

Lukes also opposes Bachrach and Baratz's formulation because of the focus on power as coterminous with conflict, even though some of their categories of power phenomena (manipulation and authority) are clearly not conflictive. In addition, putting the matter 'sharply', as Lukes (1974, p. 23) says,

> A may exercise power over B by getting him to do what he does not want to do, but he also exercises power over him by influencing, shaping or determining his very wants. Indeed, is it not the supreme exercise of power to get another or others to have the desires you want them to have—that is, to secure their compliance by controlling their thoughts and desires?

To ignore this, says Lukes (ibid.), 'is to ignore the crucial point that the most effective and insidious use of power is to prevent such conflict from arising in the first place'. It is Bachrach and Baratz's neglect of this which leads them, maintains Lukes (p. 24), to accept that, where no grievances are articulated, that a 'genuine' consensus prevails. Again, he links this to 'the supreme and most insidious exercise of power', which is

> to prevent people, to whatever degree, from having grievances by shaping their perceptions, cognitions and preferences in such a way that they accept their role in the existing order of things, either because they can see or imagine no alternative to it, or because they see it as natural and unchangeable, or because they value it as divinely ordained and beneficial? To assume that the absence of grievance equals genuine consensus is simply to rule out the possibility of false or manipulated consensus by definitional fiat (Lukes, 1974, p. 24).

Lukes takes his objections to the 'two-dimensional' view of Bachrach and Baratz to be a 'three-dimensional . . . and *thoroughgoing critique* of the *behavioural focus* of the first two views as too individualistic' (ibid.). At the same time, Lukes' analysis will allow consideration, he maintains, 'of the many ways in which *potential issues* are kept out of politics, whether through the operation of social forces and institutional practices or through individuals' decisions' (ibid.). This analysis, he maintains, will exhibit '*latent conflict*, which consists in a contradiction between the interests of those exercising power and the *real interests* of those they exclude . . . the identification of those interests ultimately always rests on empirically supportable and refutable hypotheses' (pp. 24–5).

Lukes sees the one-dimensional A-B view of power as the 'primitive notion' lying behind all talk of power, to which something additional needs to be added. This is White's (1971b) notion that A should affect B in a significant manner, which Lukes interprets as the case when 'A affects B in a manner contrary to B's interests' (Lukes, 1974, p. 27). Interests are defined by Lukes according to what he terms a 'radical' criterion, which is that which people 'would want and prefer, were they able to make the choice' (p. 34). This approach to interests and power, Lukes maintains, 'offers . . . the prospect of a serious sociological and not merely personalized explanation of how political systems prevent demands from becoming political issues or even from being made' (p. 33).

In a recent analysis of Lukes' work, Bradshaw (1976) has been highly critical of Lukes' approach. One of his points of criticism concerns Lukes' use of the notion of 'real interests', a use which he notes as one which confuses *different preferences* with real interests (Bradshaw, 1976, p. 121). Moreover, these 'different preferences' in Lukes' argument are expressed under conditions of 'relative autonomy' which are highly problematic. This is because, as Bradshaw argues, while an A may be 'relatively autonomous' in his choices *vis-à-vis* a B, he may not enjoy the same autonomy with other parties, B_1 . . . n. In addition, as Bradshaw maintains, Lukes' promotion of 'democratic participation', as the condition under which 'relative autonomy' in the choice of 'real interests' occurs, is nonsense unless conceived as something other than a part of the rhetoric of liberal-pluralist theorizing. What is wrong here is what is wrong throughout Lukes' analysis (and is also evident in Bradshaw's critique), and that is a commitment to an individualist view of power. This commitment on Lukes' part comes over clearly in his rejoinder (1976) to Bradshaw's criticism that the Lukesian concept of 'real interests' is an 'observer's assessment' made empirically rather than theoretically. Lukes (1976, p. 129), in the context of his earlier discussion of Crenson's (1971) work (see Lukes, 1974), maintains that

> I deny that my account of real interests is an 'observer's assessment'. My assumption that Gary's citizens would rather not be poisoned, had they (uncoerced) choice and adequate information, is a hypothetical prediction: if, implausibly, under such acknowledged conditions, they actually preferred continual pollution, I would abandon the claim that air pollution was against their real interests.

> The fact that in reality 'many . . . may have imagined that pollution control *would* bring on unemployment' does not show my claim to be mistaken. Suppose they were right. That merely shows that U.S. Steel would be prepared to reduce its production schedule and increase unemployment in Gary if pollution control is introduced, thereby coercing Gary's citizens and civic leaders to accept pollution. Whether right or wrong . . . the continued maintenance of this widespread belief was certainly a most potent element in U.S. Steel's power (Lukes, 1976, pp. 129–30).

Several important and revealing aspects of Lukes' (1974; 1976) analysis are evident in this extract. He clearly relates the existence of 'real interests' to individual citizens exercising 'uncoerced choice' under conditions of 'adequate information'; indeed, he even speaks of their 'preferences' in the context of a rebuttal to an attack on his position couched in the same terms as those in which he would defend it! Similarly, he reduces U.S. Steel's power, or, more correctly, 'a most potent element' of it, to individual 'citizens' and civic leaders' . . . widespread belief[s]'—in other words, to the findings of a reputational methodology! And this is supposed to be how we generate theoretical knowledge of power and structure? Rather than relying here on evidence to determine whether or not *beliefs* about U.S. Steel's preparedness 'to reduce its production schedule and increase unemployment in Gary' were justified, Lukes might instead have been concerned to argue how the *possibility* of any such beliefs, or actions, could be structurally feasible. This would imply analysis of hegemony and a mode of production, rather than agents' beliefs.

This individualist and voluntarist reliance on individuals' choices also underpins the explanation that Lukes provides of how the Community Power Debate has developed. His only explanation of it is one that links it to 'different moral and political positions' (Lukes, 1974, pp. 34–5).

Lukes' silence in this respect is what one would expect, given his commitment to an essential and underlying concept of power as being predicated on the 'one-dimensional' A-B terms that Dahl employs. How could one expand on something conceived as foundational other than by adding to it? Lukes has no conception of how the contradictions generated internally within any sociological discourse can dialectically resolve themselves, not in the harmonious building of further edifices or dimensions upon a problematic base, but through the antinomies and antitheses which the initial thesis can generate.

Dialectics of power

I would argue that debates about the concept of power in its application to local communities are not only empirical—about differing interpretations of data—but are more especially theoretic. They are theoretic in precisely the ways in which, in talking about power, the theory is power. Theory is a way of constituting social order in discourse, by making that discourse *that* discourse, something specific and rule-bound, rather than *any* discourse. I have suggested that, traditionally, in sociology, theories have been generated within the antinomies of the metaphor of a *socius-logos*, and from this have developed the antithetical tendencies of logocentrism and sociocentrism. I have characterized the Community Power Debate between Bachrach and Baratz and Dahl, for instance, as one occasion on which these antinomies display themselves. It is clear that in holding this view I am opposed to Lukes, who sees the difference between Bachrach and Baratz and Dahl as one not of dialectics, but of dimensions. One might say that where I see a deep difference, Lukes sees a deep sameness. How do I account for our difference?

Our analyses come to rest at different places. Lukes wishes to rest on the post-Hobbesian concept of power as a causal relationship between individuals, and then re-build from these foundations to a 'radical' and 'structural' view of power. I wish to treat these foundations as fictional means of resolving the myth of order. In addition, I see these fictions as themselves inscribed within a sociological framework whose rules of functioning have become almost legendary—that the purity of knowledge may reside in either a sociocentric or a logocentric realm. However, I do not regard these legendary realms as equally distant from the material world. Sociocentrism, as a strategy, is generated in a dialectical antithesis to logocentrism, and bases its moral claim to better and more authoritative utterance than the former on its stronger commitment to the material world, rather than the material world of logocentric practice, as its grounding. How do Bachrach and Baratz do this, yet at the same time remain true to Dahl's foundational speaking, as Lukes maintains?

I do not disagree with Lukes on the point that they do in fact remain within the Dahlian conventions of theorizing power as causal and individual. But I do not agree that this is in this respect the ground of their analysis. If it were, how could they ever have opposed Dahl?

It is not the way of seeing power on which they differ, but that which they will see. And, in this respect, it is not a question of competing 'views' at all, but an issue of different vistas. Bachrach and Baratz differ from Dahl not in their underlying concept of power, but in the criteria of significance which they attach to what it allows them to see, and it is in this respect that they see different things, because they point their concepts at different aspects of the material world. This is because it is not so much their concept of power, as such, which differentiates them, as the issues in which they will see it. And the criteria of what constitutes an issue are embedded in the respective *uses* to which the concept of power is put—and these uses derive, initially, from Dahl's logocentrism and from the antithetical constitution of a sociocentric framework by Bachrach and Baratz, which stretches the concept of power to its limits. These limits are the limits of its language, as a concept embedded in a language-game of action and subjectivity, as I have established in the previous chapter. Bachrach and Baratz, by attempting to transcend the limits of this language-game, *can* only succeed in stretching it to its limits. They do this by taking a concept of action—power—and attempting to deploy it in a sense which does not derive from the language-game. This is the sense of power as other than action, as, implicitly, structure. This sense of power derives not from a change in the individualist and causal basis of the concept, which remains the same, but from the difference in the issues in which it will be seen. This difference derives from the use of a sociocentric criterion of an 'issue' as that which people in the material world constitute it to be. This, in opposition to Dahl, is not a constitution of an 'issue' as that which *logos* allows it to be, but is a constitution of it as that which ordinary *socius* allows it to be.

In the absence of the fiction of a *Leviathan* in the social world, then social theory can only create that order which it is. Hence, logocentric theory creates an order which is of its own making, in seeing its methodological stipulations *reflected* in the social world (here one may refer to an earlier formulation of this theme in Clegg, 1975, pp. 17–30). Similarly, sociocentrism seeks not to find correspondence in the social world with its stipulations, but stipulates the social world as that with which it will *cohere*. Hence the reliance on 'decision-making' (about *its* decisions) in the material world as logocentrism's source of data, and socio-centrism's reliance on what people say they think—the 'reputational approach'. Typically, and I think that one probably cannot put it any stronger, each method has generated a 'view' of power distinctively different from that of the other. Each of these views—which characterize power as either plurally dispersed or as centralized in an élite—poses a solution to the problem generated by the absence of *Leviathan* in the presence of a causal, individualist concept of power. The characterization of power as pluralist theorizes order in the absence of *Leviathan* through making each person, as a group member, a sovereign entity over something, somewhere, on some occasions. As each group that exists has some sovereignty, no one group is wholly sovereign, particularly as the scope of sovereignty varies from group to group. Hence order is the result of different alliances between different factional groups, with differentiated sovereignty, at different points in time and space. The characterization of power as élitist theorizes order in the absence of *Leviathan* through elevating particular persons and groups to the role of an unofficial *Leviathan*. Thus has order been theorized through power.

If the concept of power as embedded in a language-game of human agency and action reaches its limits with Bachrach and Baratz, where does it go with Lukes?

Little further. Lukes attempts to make it go further in that he wants his third-dimensional view to be able to incorporate 'social forces and institutional practices' (Lukes, 1974, p. 24), and he proposes doing this through a study of 'real interests'. But he has no theoretical way of identifying 'real interests' and has to fall back on empirical criteria constructed with reference to the preferences of a homunculus 'exercising choice under conditions of relative autonomy' (Lukes, 1974, p. 33), which become visible when constituted comparatively under the rubric of J. S. Mill's 'canon of difference'. (Lukes takes Crenson's (1971) empirical study of *The Un-Politics of Air Pollution: A Study of Non-Decisionmaking in the Cities* as an example of this.)

The deficiencies in this approach become only too evident when Lukes (1974, p. 50) discusses 'peculiarly acute problems' in identifying 'the process or mechanism of an alleged exercise of power, on the three-dimensional view', in particular the problems of 'unconsciousness' and 'collectivities'. Lukes' (p. 51) whole discussion of 'How can power be exercised without the exerciser being aware of what he (it) is doing?' is couched in terms of agents' awareness of what they do, or do not do, which, given the grammar of power, is as one would expect. However, Lukes has no conception of the limits of this language and can only offer the 'fact' of this power-agency linkage, rather than make it problematic. Tied to this is his juxtaposition of power and structure as mutually exclusive. Hence, as Cox (1976) argues, Lukes has no alternative other than to make structure residual to his concept of power and thus attempt to incorporate it into his general concept of power—but this is something which he has already negated the possibility of doing by making of his commitment to the Hobbesian-Dahlian fiction of power *all* of his commitment to power. Lukes wishes to distinguish between 'structural determination' and the exercise of power, and hence can only refer to collectivity power in terms of aggregated agents responsibly choosing their actions, where choice is available to them.

Lukes remains within the grammar of power, but seeks to extend it beyond its use in the discourse (as shown in chapter 2), in order to extend Bachrach and Baratz's discussion of power and non-decisions into a conception of power *and* structure. But, having made Dahl's fiction foundational, he has to remain within the limits of this analysis, while paradoxically attempting to breach these limits.

While I have argued that Lukes may be said to be unable to transcend the grammar of power, Lukes has said much the same of Poulantzas in the context of the grammar of 'structures'. Lukes cites Poulantzas as a theoretical instance of someone who theorizes power, not as power (i.e. in terms of its grammar), but as *structural determination*. Lukes formulates the problem thus:

> when can social causation be characterized as an exercise of power, or, more precisely, how and where is the line to be drawn between structural determination on the one hand, and an exercise of power, on the other? This is a problem which has often reappeared in the history of Marxist thought, in the context of discussions of determinism and voluntarism. Thus, for example, within post-war French Marxism, an extreme determinist position is adopted by the structuralist Marxism of Louis Althusser and his followers, as opposed to the so-called 'humanist', 'historicist' and 'subjectivist' interpretations of thinkers such as Sartre and Lucien Goldmann, and behind them of Lukács and Korsch (and, behind them, of Hegel), for whom the historical 'subject' has a crucial and ineradicable explanatory role. For Althusser, Marx's thought, properly understood, conceptualizes 'the determination of the elements of a whole by the structure of the whole', and 'liberated definitively from the empiricist antinomies of phenomenal subjectivity and essential interiority', treats of 'an objective system governed, in its most concrete determinations, by the laws of its *arrangement* (montage)

and of its *machinery*, by the specifications of its concept' (Lukes, 1974, p. 52; citations from Althusser and Balibar, 1968, pp. 63, 71).

Lukes argues that this structural determination is not amenable to the grammar of power, and that therefore it is not possible to discuss power at all within Poulantzas' (1973) discourse:

> To use the vocabulary of power in the context of social relationships is to speak of human agents, separately or together, in groups or organizations, through action or inaction, significantly affecting the thoughts or action of others (specifically, in a manner contrary to their interests). In speaking thus, one assumes that, although the agents operate within structurally determined limits, they nonetheless have a certain relative autonomy and could have acted differently . . . within a system characterized by total structural determinism, there would be no place for power (Lukes, 1974, pp. 54–5).

No place, that is, unless one stipulates a redefinition of power in terms of structural determination, which is what Lukes (1974, p. 55) maintains Poulantzas does. And so, with Mills (1959), Lukes appears to conclude 'in favour of attributing power to those in strategic positions who are able to initiate changes that are in the interests of broad segments of society but do not' (Lukes, 1974, p. 56).

In summary, one might characterize Lukes' (1974) analysis as one in which morally responsible agents choose their actions under conditions of more or less relative autonomy. These individuals inhabit a space somewhere between fate and freedom, in external and contingent relationship with structures and institutions of social organization. As Jessop (1976, p. 12) remarks, in Lukes' analysis

> The complex relations between social actors and social constraints are necessarily seen in terms of a mechanical, additive model—social structure imposes certain limits on possible outcomes at a given time and, within these limits, individuals (seen as distinct unitary subjects inserted into the given situation) are free to choose their course of action and thus determine that one particular possibility is realised for the moment . . . men are situated at the interface of two worlds, the determined and the contingent, the realm of causation and the realm of reason. It is their responsibility to choose whether to act in the interests of broad segments of society or to advance their own selfish interests.

And so 'a radical view' of power concludes by identifying itself with the free and rational actions of concrete individuals. If this reliance on the problematic of the subject, and the ideology of liberalism, is Lukes' view of the 'radical', then I would argue that it must be concluded that this view is insufficient, precisely inasmuch as it represents, however innocently, what I have termed the 'fictions' of Hobbes' analysis of power. Thus, I would say that the use of Lukes' 'view' of power is that it enables us to see the outer limits of an historical grammar in which power has been conceptualized as part of the grammar of action. It reaches these limits in its attempt to assimilate structure to power. This attempt can only be ceded to be 'radical' if one is not aware of the grammar which articulates it, and which it articulates. Ironically, this is evidenced in Lukes' text as early as the title page. *Power: A Radical View* already carries within it a significant antinomy. This is the idea that *a view*—that which appears to be the case, that which presents itself to vision, that which is on the surface and can thus be seen—can be *radical*. As in its usage in botany, that which is radical is of or on the root: it is basic, grounding and original. Lukes never questions basics, grounds, origins or roots, and merely builds a two- and three-dimensional superstructure upon an unquestioned and unexplored foundation.

Chapter 5
Structure and power

Parsons, power and structure

Within the liberal-individualist mode of theorizing power, attempts have been made to develop more structural concepts of power as something which one can not only exercise, but also possess.

It is the distinction between the 'having' and the 'exercising' of power which Van den Bergh (1972, p. 3) formulates as the source of a fallacy. This fallacy, he proposes, is 'the idea that power is a kind of *substance* that one can *have* in one's pocket in the same way as money.' This fallacy has a number of illustrious promoters, among them Deutsch (1963; 1968) and Parsons (1967).

As Baldwin (1971, p. 579) states, most comparisons between 'power' in political theory and 'money' in economic theory rarely develop much beyond the level of rhetoric and metaphor. He identifies Catlin's (1927) usage as an exception to this tendency. Catlin's (1927, p. 579) proposal is to found the study of politics on as rigorous a basis as the study of economics, through the 'establishment of a standard and unit of value'. Perhaps the most well-known development of such a programme is Parsons' (1967), of which Deutsch (1963, p. 116) exclaims that it 'has perhaps opened a path to a more fundamental reinterpretation of power than has been possible since the days of Hobbes and Locke'.

Parsons (1967, p. 297) proposes that his treatment of power will offer:

> a promising way to deal with certain of the most baffling difficulties that have dogged the analysis of power in the literature of political theory. Foremost among these difficulties were the problem of specificity of conceptualization as compared with the diffuseness of conceptions which virtually equate power with all forms of capacity to gain ends (the Hobbesian approach), the problem of the relations between the coercive and consensual aspects of power systems, the problem of the balance between the hierarchical aspects of power and the existence of egalitarian elements in the structure of political systems, and finally, what is sometimes called the 'zero-sum'

problem, that of whether any relational system necessarily contains only a fixed amount of power which is subject only to redistribution.

Parsons (1967, p. 299) expressly wishes to treat 'power as a *specific* mechanism operating to bring about changes in the action of other units, individual or collective, in the process of social interaction'. To do this he makes a number of initial and general assumptions concerning the alleged 'parallelism in theoretical structure between the conceptual schemes appropriate for the analysis of the economic and the political aspects of societies' (ibid.). This 'parallelism' is of four kinds.

The first parallel is that Parsons' view of the 'political' is of an analytical, abstract and generalized phenomenon which can be dealt with by a political theory composed of a 'conceptual scheme . . . a restricted set of primary variables and their interrelations . . . operating in all concrete parts of social systems' (Parsons, 1967, p. 300). The scene of these operations is the 'polity', considered by Parsons to be a further parallel, this time with the 'economy'. Within this 'polity' the 'political process' is that 'by which the necessary organization is built up and operated, the goals of action are determined and the resources requisite to it are mobilized' (p. 301). In the polity, just as in the economy, Parsons sees 'demand', 'consumers', 'resource mobilization' and the 'creative combination' of 'factors of production'. 'Demand' in the economy is paralleled by the 'goal-demands'—what we might call the agenda—of interest groups in the polity. Finally, power is regarded as 'a generalized medium in a sense directly parallel in logical structure . . . to money as the generalized medium of the economic process. . . . Power then is generalized capacity to secure the performance of binding obligations' (pp. 301, 308).

As Giddens (1968, p. 260) observes, Parsons' power is 'directly derivative of authority; authority is the institutionalized legitimation which underlies power'. Thus, there is no such thing as 'illegitimate power', for such an action would not, could not, be power, but would be 'intrinsic instrumentality', one of the several ways in which one may 'get things done', ranging from 'force' to 'conscience'. Power, unlike 'force', is a phenomenon which is 'generated' by the social system from its 'central value system', as a way of achieving the collective goals that this value system stipulates. Hence, the legitimacy of power: it is simply a socially sanctioned means for achieving socially sanctioned ends. Because this legitimacy is founded on trust and confidence—as is the monetary system of exchange—it can be regarded as an investment which returns dividends in the achievement of collective goals. The criticism has been made that

> what slips away from sight almost completely in the Parsonian analysis is the very fact that power, even as Parsons defines it, is always exercised over someone! By treating power as necessarily (by definition) legitimate, and thus *starting* from the assumption of consensus of some kind between power-holders and those subordinate to them, Parsons virtually ignores, quite consciously and deliberately, the necessarily hierarchical character of power, and the divisions of interest which are frequently consequent upon it. However much it is true that power can rest upon 'agreement' to cede authority which can be used for collective aims, it is also true that interests of power-holders and those subject to that power often clash. It is undoubtedly the case that some 'zero-sum' (coercion) theories tend to argue as if power differentials *inevitably* curtail conflicts of interest, and produce overt conflicts—and fail to give sufficient attention to specifying the conditions under which no conflict of either type is present. But it is surely beyond dispute that positions of power offer to their incumbents definite material and psychological rewards, and thereby stimulate conflicts between those who want power, and those who have it. . . . To have power is to have potential access to valued scarce resources, and thus power *itself* becomes a scarce resource (Giddens, 1968, pp. 264, 265).

Giddens locates Parsons' analysis clearly within the consensus/order axis of a now largely irrelevant debate. It is because of this counterposing of 'consensus' to the seamy realism of 'conflict' that one might neglect in Giddens' interpretation of Parsons the importance of consensus as an achieved phenomenon of power itself. Parsons' use of the concepts of 'authority' and 'bindingness' do serve to justify the use of power, by embedding it in an institutionalized normative code, as Giddens observes. In addition, Parsons does, albeit in an atomistic manner, indicate that consensus can be regarded as an outcome of the power phenomenon, rather than just the condition of its existence. This distinction is made when Parsons indicates that power is not only to be considered as exercised when an A ('ego') can manipulate B's ('alter's') situation, but may also occur when

> without attempting to change alter's situation, ego may attempt to change alter's intentions, ie, he may manipulate symbols which are meaningful to alter in such a way that he tries to make alter 'see' that what ego wants is a 'good thing' for him (alter) to do (Parsons, 1967, p. 309).

This implies that any achieved consensus, authority or binding obligation within which power is exercised 'legitimately' may itself be an achieved phenomenon, and thus, in itself, the result of power. But such an implication would itself imply that the reading of Parsons which could justify such an interpretation, would be one not confined to the conventions of Parsons' text, in which symbols are themselves manipulated, rather than manipulating.

An alternative reading would be one that, instead of regarding meaningful symbols such as language as some sort of medium of exchange between ego's and alter's, which may be manipulated at will, would see language as something which in-itself structured some other phenomena such as 'intentions'. Otherwise the idea of intentions as somehow independent of meaningful symbols such as language seems quite odd. Could one change one's intentions and not change one's language? Clearly, one could not, if one is referring to the language-in-use with which one would or could formulate an intention. In so far as another's intentions are a mystery to us unless *we* speculate on *them*, or they are *declared* to us (through speech or action—the conventions of either), the interest in intentions must always be one which is pre-eminently an interest in the conventions of communication.

Giddens, like Parsons, 'tends to accept the operations of authority at their face-value' (Giddens, 1968, p. 267). The face that Giddens focuses on is simply more obscured, by being further backstage, than that of the front-stage puppets whom he sees being manipulated by these 'behind-the-scenes' persons. While 'the puppeteers behind the scenes may be the people who hold real control' (p. 267), the sociological question is not just to expose their features, but also to make apparent how these relationships are possible; '*how legitimation is mediated in its operation in systems of power*' (p. 269).

Giddens, power and structure

Giddens (1976), following a route remarkably similar to one followed elsewhere a little earlier (Clegg, 1975), attempts to address this problem through the synthesis of concepts of 'action' and 'structure', 'meaning' and 'power'. Giddens (1976, p. 19) proposes the synthesis of 'the social (and linguistic) foundation of reflexivity, such as was independently arrived at from widely varying perspectives, by Mead, Wittgenstein, and Heidegger—and, following the latter, Gadamer' as one of more significance than that which Parsons traces and grounds his project in, the 'internalization of values' in Durkheim and Freud.

Both Giddens (1976) and Clegg (1975) attempt to reconcile what have hitherto been two divergent, and frequently opposed, types of discourse. One of these is the traditional sociological mainstream positivist-functionalist interest in *rules* as 'properties of collectivities'. This interest has most frequently been expressed in a logocentric framework. It is because of this that the necessarily socially constituted and reconstituted, produced and reproduced, nature of rule as a reflexive members' practice has been neglected. The import of this treatment of the concept of rule is visible in post-Wittgensteinian philosophy, in terms of what I have called a sociocentric interest. A typical corollary of this interest has been a tendency to accept members' practices as in-themselves reflexive, *but* in a way which, while it might stress the mediation of speech/language in daily life, has, in doing so, neglected the mediation of this speech/language as *praxis* occurring in definite structural circumstances. This is, in part, because it has neglected the reflexive *theoretical* mediation which would make such a grasp of everyday life/language apprehensible not only as a scene of action, but also as one which is, in a large part, a *ruled, determinate* and *dominated structural scene*. This is not to obviate the possibility of *action* as *action*, as creative and willed, but is to stress that this action is a realm of freedom inscribed within a realm of necessity, *a realm of proscribed and prescribed possibilities*.

Where sociologists have sought an alternative to the 'Durksonian' (Bauman, 1976) tradition, in which rules are external and constraining to the active agency of the person in social action, then, as Giddens (1976, p. 98) notes, they have usually looked to Marx. He cites Dahrendorf, Lockwood and Rex as examples, and argues that none of these authors has engaged in either a sufficient critique of Parsons or in a sufficient 'borrowing' from Marx, who emphasizes man as producer and creator. Having criticized Parsons (Giddens, 1968), he will now 'borrow' from Marx (Giddens, 1976).

He observes 'that there are few clear ties drawn in Marx's own writings between the conception of social man as *homo faber*, which forms the general background to his theory of history, and the more specific analyses that he offered of class formations and class conflict' (Giddens, 1976, p. 99). Giddens attributes this to the fact that the 'philosophical anthropology' of Marx's earlier work, in particular of the *1844 Manuscripts* (1973a), 'remains latent in Marx's subsequent works' (p. 100). Consequently,

> Marx's use of the concepts supposedly involved in 'coercion theory'—material interest, conflict and power—are worked out in . . . the historical interpretation and development of particular types of society via the concept of modes of production, division of labour, private property and classes, concentrating of course upon the critique of political economy and the optative transformation of capitalism by socialism . . . the only cogent analyses of conflict and power in Marx link those specifically with class interests (Giddens, 1976, pp. 101–2).

Giddens notes that, because of this 'rupture' in Marx's works, and because of the lack of continuity of his 'philosophical anthropology' in the later works, these texts 'do not provide an elaborated alternative' to the 'Durksonian' (Bauman, 1976) stress on 'value, norm and convention' (Giddens, 1976, p. 102).

Giddens proposes to construct such an 'elaborated alternative' which will rely upon the mature Marx's 'fundamental idea of *the production and re-production of social life*'. This 'idea' will have 'to be understood in a very broad sense', warns Giddens, such that 'in order to detail its implications we have to go well beyond what is immediately available in Marx's works' (Giddens, 1976, p. 102). 'Going beyond' Marx's works, in this instance, turns out to be a use of Marx's metaphors of 'production and re-production' in the context of, not *material*, but *social* life.

Giddens' understanding of Marx's concept of 'production' is as the 'reproduction of structures of interaction', inasmuch as it is the reflexivity of language 'which is above all the *medium of human practical activities*' (Giddens, 1976, p. 103). Giddens is thus concerned to separate the production and reproduction of material life from the production and reproduction of 'social life', so as to focus on the latter. He develops his analysis 'with reference to language . . . because language, as a social form itself, exemplifies some aspects—and only some aspects—of social life as a whole' (ibid.). He goes on to distinguish 'three aspects' of the analysis of language in its production and reproduction, 'each of which is characteristic of the production and reproduction of society more generally' (ibid.). These are the following:

> Language is 'mastered' and 'spoken' by actors; it is employed as a medium of communication between them; and it forms a 'structure'

which is in some sense constituted by the speech of a 'language community' or collectivity (Giddens, 1976, p. 103).

It is on this basis that Giddens proposes to treat 'social life . . . as a set of *reproduced practices*', entailing analysis of 'social practices . . . from the point of view of their constitution as a series of *acts*, "brought off" by actors; second, as constituting forms of *interaction*, involving the communication of meaning; and third, as constituting *structures* which pertain to "collectivities" or "social communities"' (Giddens, 1976, p. 104). It is the latter two levels of analysis in particular, those of 'interaction' and 'structures', that Giddens will analyse in their 'mediation . . . in processes of social re-production' (p. 122; this gives rise to a diagrammatic representation which the reader may wish to compare with Clegg, 1975, p. 78).

What Giddens' analysis of the level of interaction involves is, quite simply, a marriage between an ethnomethodological stress on 'interpretative schemes' (Giddens, 1976, p. 107) and a conception of these as 'moral orders of interaction' in which both 'enabling' and 'constraining' rules operate as 'rights' and 'obligations' (p. 108; again, the reader may wish to compare this with Clegg, 1975, pp. 75–6). These together constitute an 'order' which is 'negotiated'. This 'negotiated order' represents the 'asymmetrically interdependent . . . moral co-ordination of interaction' as meaningfully produced, 'with its expression of relations of power' (Giddens, 1976, p. 110).

What concept of power is Giddens operating with here? It proves to be one which is 'logically tied' to the 'notion of action':

> Action intrinsically involves the application of 'means' to achieve outcomes, brought about through the direct intervention of an actor in a course of events, 'intended action' being a sub-class of the actor's doings, or his refraining from doing; power represents the capacity of the agent to mobilize resources to constitute those 'means'. In this most general sense, 'power' refers to the *transformative capacity* of human action . . . [which is] the capability of the actor to intervene in a series of events so as to alter their course; as such it is the 'can' which mediates between intentions or wants and the actual realization of the outcomes sought after. 'Power' in the narrower, relational sense is a property of interaction, and may be defined as the capability to secure outcomes where the realization of these outcomes depends upon the agency of *others*. It is in this sense that men have power 'over' others; this is power as domination (Giddens, 1976, pp. 110–11).

In view of the conceptual priority which Giddens places on 'power', a concept 'logically tied' to social action, in preference to 'domination', which he is shortly to deploy as a 'structural' corollary to the 'interaction' concept of power, *then domination is grounded in, and made dependent upon, power.* (Or perhaps he is simply equivocal here—the rather unspecific double-headed arrow of the diagrammatic representation on p. 122 of his model would seem to suggest as much.) It is because of this that it is no surprise to find that Giddens' analysis is located within an excessively 'humanistic problematic' of an Hegelian emphasis on action, rather than being dialecticized in fusion with a more materialist conception of the properties of action as themselves an 'effect of the structures in the field of social relations' (Poulantzas, 1973, p. 64). Despite his use of the metaphors of 'production and reproduction', this overtly Hegelian formulation was already implicit in his espousal of a 'philosophical anthropology' in which *the subject, in social life*, was predominant.

In this respect, although it is couched in terms of quite different concepts and references, it is no surprise to find that Giddens' analysis comes to rest at exactly the same point as Lukes', although through a different process of thought. While Giddens makes both logocentrism and sociocentrism problematic, he does not make power problematic. That is, he does not appear to realize the contradictions inherent in taking a concept of social action as *foundational* for a concept of social structure. This is what is implied in his constitution of a property of *structures—* domination—as *dependent* upon a property of *action*. It is in this respect, above all others, that Giddens (1976) and Clegg (1975) differ. This difference is crucial: it is what enables Giddens (p. 113) to write that ' "what passes for social reality" stands in immediate relation to the distribution of power', where one might have added that 'what passes for the distribution of power' stands in immediate relation to 'social reality'.

This difference is further indexed by Giddens' (p. 111, pp. 116–18) unproblematic concept of 'intentions' and 'wants'. As I have already argued and as I will elaborate at greater length in the following chapter, in the context of Abell's (1976) work, the 'intentions' or 'wants' of the actor cannot be assumed to be a secure basis for the presumption of analysis into power, because they cannot be constituted independently of broader, structural aspects of power phenomena—such as domination—unless one makes the mistake of theorizing these as conceptually generated from this level in the first place.

Perhaps I am being too critical of Giddens—certainly, he is equivocal enough at crucial instances for this to be all too easy; it is difficult to criticize satisfactorily work which appears to be unclear as to the level at which it is operative. For instance, Giddens, having told us on page 111 that 'domination' is a relational concept of power and hence a subsidiary concept of social action, proposes on page 122 that domination is a property of structures; yet we are also told

> that structures are 'subject-less'. Interaction is constituted by and in the conduct of subjects; *structuration*, as the reproduction of practices, refers abstractly to the dynamic process whereby structures come into being. By the *duality of structure* I mean that social structures are both constituted *by* human agency, and yet at the same time are the very *medium* of this constitution. . . . What I call 'modalities' refer to the mediation of interaction and structure in processes of social reproduction. . . . The communication of meaning in interaction involves the use of interpretative schemes by means of which sense is *made* by participants of what each says and does. The appreciation of such cognitive schemes, within a framework of mutual knowledge, depends upon and draws from a 'cognitive order' which is shared by a community; but while drawing upon such a cognitive order the application of interpretative schemes at the same time *reconstitutes* that order. *The use of power in interaction involves the application of facilities whereby participants are able to generate outcomes through affecting the conduct of others; the facilities are both drawn from an order of domination and at the same time, as they are applied, reproduce that order of domination* (my emphasis). Finally, the moral constitution of interaction involves the application of norms which draw from a legitimate order, and yet by that very application reconstitute it. Just as communication, power and morality are integral elements of interaction, so signification, domination and legitimation are only analytically separable properties of structure (Giddens, 1976, pp. 121; 122–3).

Despite the talk of structures and structuration, the whole basis of the schema is *individualist* and *voluntarist*, as I have attempted to demonstrate through the emphasis (in italics) that I have given to *the individualist formulation of power* and *the voluntarist formulation of domination as a source of facilities*.

Taken together like this, it would appear that the key to the 'duality of structures' must be the acting individual 'drawing' from, and 'reproducing', 'that order of domination'.

Such voluntarism has little to do with a Marxist theory, in which, in concrete empirical instances, the situation is characterized not by a circular Hegelian totality in which the acting subject objectifies equivalent elements (power and domination), but by a 'complex structure *in* dominance' (Poulantzas, 1973, p. 38; my emphasis). Domination *is*. It is not something one 'draws from'. At the level of concrete historical analysis of specific social formations, 'the theoretically constructed concept of a mode of production' is 'a complex whole in dominance' (Poulantzas, 1973, p. 41), and as such is not a concept of contingent choice. One cannot choose what dominates one, other than through concerted class praxis as a revolutionary way of reformulating dominance.

However, both Lukes (1974) and Giddens (1976) arrive at a point quite contrary to this. Each wants to talk about power *and* structure, but each ends up talking mainly about power; each subsumes structure to power (although this is less clear in Giddens than in Lukes). Both theorists achieve their synthesis of 'power' and 'structure' through making their theoretical movement from the level of appearances as given. Each treats this 'market-place' of power-relations, the moment of exchange, as fundamental to the analysis of social structure, without realizing that this is rather like treating money simply in its obvious form as a circulatory medium, its appearance, without relating its appearance to that which makes it possible: value (Marx, 1974, chs. 3 and 5). It is to move from the concrete to the abstract, rather than from the abstract to the concrete. It is to leave the relationship between acting human subjects and the possibilities of their exercise, *or* having, of power, as untheorized. This is because the analyses never move outside the problematic fiction of power; even in Giddens' more sophisticated analysis, there is a constant vacillation between formulations which suggest (1) that 'structures' are 'mastered' by actors ('Language is "mastered" and "spoken" by actors'; Giddens, 1976; p. 103) and (2) that actors are mastered by structures which they 'constitute', but which, as the 'medium' of constitution, constrain them (p. 121). I am not objecting to dialectics here, but to dialectics without any specific determination. It is unclear what, in what circumstances, would determine what masters whom, or who masters what. *This is because of the absence of any theoretical formulation in Giddens of the concept of domination in and as structure, or in Lukes of issues and interests, in and through structure*. The ground of this failure of analysis is their respective inability to free structure from the fiction of the subject in their theoretical work. What is necessary is to produce theoretical work in which, in this instance, concepts of power and structure, of power and domination, and of power, issues and interests, can be determinately related in ways which are both necessarily predictable and explicable within the scope of the theory and plausible within the scope of whatever empirical material they may discuss.

Essentially, these questions reduce to just one: how to theorize power as a concept of social action, and thus as a possibility of its historical grammar, yet also as a concept of social structure, in order to extend it to the point beyond its grammar where recent critiques would have it go?

These are issues of contemporary Marxist analysis.

Chapter 6
Marxist analyses of power and structure

It is a frequently acknowledged fact that neither Marx nor subsequent Marxist theorists have produced a specific theory of power or of politics (e.g., Anderson, 1976, pp. 44–5, refers to the 'studied silence of Western Marxism' *vis-à-vis* 'analysis of the political machinery of the bourgeois state'; see also Poulantzas, 1973, pp. 21, 99). Despite this, some Marxist theorists have attempted to develop a political theory out of Marx's work. Notable amongst these attempts in its relevance for a theory of power is the work of Nicos Poulantzas. There is neither the space nor the necessity in this work to provide a full account and analysis of his contribution to Marxist analysis. Instead, I will concentrate on the issue of dispute which Lukes (1974) makes with Poulantzas: that of structural determination.

Poulantzas (1973) argues that a theory of power can be read into the constitution of the field of class practices. Thus, for Poulantzas (1973, p. 99) the concept of power must be related to a Marxist concept of class from which certain conclusions can be drawn, 'regarding the problem of relations between power and social classes'. These are that the concept of power specifies the effects of the whole ensemble of levels of structure on agents involved at these levels in social relationships between classes in struggle. Power is an effect of the ensemble of levels of structure, where structures are analysed as de-centred totalities. Such totalities derive their specific form from the articulation of several structures within the social formation. Each of these has a certain relative autonomy and a specific effect on the overall social formation in which it is embedded.

Poulantzas (1973, p. 99) does not assimilate class to power, or power to class, despite emphatically stating that '*class relations are relations of power*'. Neither concept is the foundation of the other, but each is constituted within the common 'field bounded by social relations', such that

> Class relations are no more the foundation of power relations than power relations are the foundations of class relations. Just as the

concept of class points to the effects of the ensemble of the levels of the structure on the supports, so the concept of power specifies the effects of the ensemble of these levels on the relations between social classes in struggle. *It points to the effects of the structure on the relations of conflict between the practices of the various classes in 'struggle'.* In other words, power is not located in the levels of structures, but is an effect of the ensemble of these levels, while at the same time characterizing each of the levels of class struggle (Poulantzas, 1973, pp. 99–100).

Poulantzas goes on to say that 'the concept of power cannot thus be applied to one level of the structure' but only to a 'determinate class' to whose interests the level of the structure corresponds. This formulation of power is that which Lukes (1974) characterizes as 'an extreme determinist position', in which there is 'no place' for power. Jessop (1976), who provides a succinct summary of the Poulantzian complexities, denies Lukes' assertion concerning Poulantzas' concept of power: he argues (p. 20) that

> It does not follow . . . that class power is totally determined by (and thus reducible to a simple epiphenomenon of) the ensemble of structures. All it implies is that, in contrast to relations of might or force (*puissance*) where the position of those involved is independent of their differential place in the overall process of production (as in cases of friendship), relations of power are relations between classes whose situation is determined by their members' specific function in production. However, . . . power relations . . . also reveal qualities that are not directly determined by this ensemble . . . while the latter does indeed impose limits (*qua* effects) on the realization of class interests, it does *not* totally determine the capacity to pursue such interests. This capacity also depends on the economic, political and ideological organization of each class and thus on the exact relation of social forces involved in the class struggle. In short, the effective political power of a class is determined through a double delimitation—through the limits imposed as effects of the complex articulation of the various structural levels of a social formation and, within these constraints, the limits involved in the relations between different class practices in the field of economic, political and ideological struggle. Strictly speaking, power is identical with these limits in the second degree. And, in turn, the effectiveness of the ensemble of structures on the field of practices is itself limited by the intervention of class struggles on the articulation of different levels of the social formation.

Jessop's analysis presents some noteworthy advances over either Lukes' (1974) or Giddens' (1976) work on power. It locates itself neither wholly at the level of action nor wholly at the level of structures. Both agents and structures can have specific historically analysable effectiveness. The most significant advance in this form of analysis is, that power is defined not in terms of social action or relationships, but *in terms of its effects within a structural context*. This leads Jessop (1976, p. 22) to define 'power' thus:

> Power is exercised when subjects engage in practices that produce effects on other subjects that, giving the prevailing combinations of structural constraints and social forces, would not otherwise have occurred.

Jessop (p. 22) states that it is 'theoretical practice that defines the terms and level of analysis and thus determines the inclusion or exclusion of specific actions and consequences in a given study'. This does not explicitly state how one should construct this theoretical practice, other than (p. 23) that 'it is essential to show how the agents' capacities and ideological formation combine with "structural" constraints and other factors to produce a given effect'. Hence, power is not equivalent to structural determination, but is the result of an overdetermination by a number of structural and conjunctural factors. Hence, it is necessary to develop differentiated concepts for relating different 'structural constraints and social forces' at different levels of structure to different agents within the social formation, or element of it. These concepts must be analytically integrated within an overall theoretical framework if we are not to be reduced to the empirical impotence of behavioural scientists such as Dahl, for whom comparative analysis is almost impossible, except in 'stable systems with recurrent routines between immutable members', as I have argued elsewhere (Clegg, 1975, pp. 22–3).

Differentiated concepts at different levels of analysis

I have argued that Lukes' attempt to articulate the concept of power over the range of power and structure is an attempt to extend concepts of action into areas in which their grammar is not at home. As I demonstrated in chapter 4, this type of articulation constantly leads the concept of power to the limits of its language. It is necessary to articulate the limits and potential of this grammar within a context which is capable of embedding the analysis of power within the analysis of structures, as Jessop (1976) indicates.

The necessary task is to articulate concepts at the structural level, which can explain the emergence and non-emergence of issues and interests, and their relationship at the level of action. What this implies is some theoretical criteria of the significance and rationality of those issues and interests which are evident in both social action and inaction, and some way of specifying how and why these theoretical criteria should be acceded to. This entails three levels of analysis: the levels of structure, mediation and action.

Concepts are available for specification at the three levels of analysis, in both the Weberian corpus and the Marxist corpus, particularly the work of Gramsci. It is from the former that both Giddens (1976) and Clegg (1975) developed their concepts of structural 'domination', although the latter work attempted to combine this understanding of domination as a structural concept with an understanding of Wittgenstein (1968) on 'form of life', in order to show why the structural level of analysis was not just one more of '*n* levels' of analysis, but the 'deepest' level. In this respect the concept of 'form of life' articulates a similar role to that of the concept of 'mode of life' in Marx and Engels' (1965) *The German Ideology*, or the concept of 'hegemony' in Gramsci's (1971) *Prison Notebooks*. With such a multiplicity of concepts operative at the structural level of domination, it is necessary to specify them in the particulars of their use.

I have discussed Weber (and Simmel) at length elsewhere (Clegg, 1975, ch. 4), and it will suffice here to point out that it is clearly Weber who provides the resources for not only my own interpretation of 'domination', but also Giddens', and that, although our accounts of the concept differ, this is not because of any lack of faithfulness to Weber on either of our parts. Rather it is the case that Weber's (1968) own analysis is equivocal, an equivocality which I have interpreted as arising from Weber's use of the concept of *Herrschaft* in two distinct contexts. One of these concepts translates as *legitimate domination*, or *authority*, which is an aspect of the individualist grammar of power: 'the probability that a command with a given specific content will be obeyed by a given group of persons' (Weber, 1968, p. 53). This use need not detain us. In addition, Weber (pp. 217–26, 941–2) also discusses *Herrschaft* as a formal concept. This may be interpreted as the formal concept of domination (Clegg, 1975, pp. 59–62), experienced in terms of differing substantive types of rule as its content. Simmel (1971, p. 116) argues that the specific content of this formal concept of domination is given by 'an objective principle' regarded by those subordinated to it as 'a concrete object (which) governs the domination'. For Weber (1968, p. 942) this 'objective principle' in the 'most important' cases, and the 'vast majority', utilizes 'economic power'.

This is not to say that domination *is* economic power, but that economic power is an important determinant of domination, albeit one which is not wholly determinant.

There are ways of formulating this from a Marxist perspective. One way would be in terms of domination as 'mode' or 'form of life'. A second would be in the analytic terms of the concept of hegemony, while the third would be through the concept of 'mode of production'. I will proceed on the assumption that none of these different emphases is sufficient by itself. Each has to be taken with the others, as interpenetrating the others, with, in Althusser's (1969, p. 111) terms, *determination in the last instance by the (economic) mode of production* of *'the relative autonomy of the superstructures and their specific effectivity'*. In these terms, it is to the 'superstructure' of 'hegemony', that, as consciousness, the role of reproducing the mode of production in and through the daily routines of everyday life, will analytically belong. And, as Althusser (p. 113) maintains, the superstructural level as the site of 'the *accumulation of effective determinations*' itself effects '*the determination in the last instance by the economic*'.

Althusser observes that 'the theory of the specific effectivity of the superstructures and other "circumstances" largely remains to be elaborated' (p. 113). He 'can only think of Gramsci' as one who 'has *really* attempted to follow up the explorations of Marx and Engels' in this area (p. 114). In this context he suggests that Gramsci's concept of 'hegemony' would be useful in the construction of such a theory.

Gramsci and hegemony

Gramsci's (1971) use of the concept of 'hegemony' is embedded in both a specific context in the development of Marxism and a specific function in its contemporary discourse. The 'strange history' of these texts, as Piccone (1976, p. 488) puts it, has been interpreted in a number of works such as Piccone (1976), Davidson (1974) and, most recently and exhaustively, Anderson (1977).

The 'strange history' of Gramsci's texts has had the consequence of producing them as work censored three times in the course of their becoming the texts we now know. Initially, as Anderson puts it,

> Gramsci underwent the normal fate of original theorists, from which neither Marx nor Lenin was exempt: the necessity of working towards radically new concepts in an old vocabulary, designed for other purposes and times, which overlaid and deflected their meaning. Just as Marx had to think many of his innovations in the language of Hegel or Smith, Lenin in that of Plekhanov and Kautsky, so Gramsci often had to produce his concepts within the archaic and inadequate apparatus of Croce or Machiavelli. This familiar problem, however, is compounded by the fact that Gramsci wrote in prison, under atrocious conditions, with a fascist censor scrutinizing everything that he produced. The involuntary disguise that inherited language so often imposes on a pioneer was thus superimposed by a voluntary disguise which Gramsci assumed to evade his jailers. The result is a work censored twice over: its spaces, ellipses, contradictions, disorders, allusions, repetitions, are the result of this uniquely adverse process of composition (Anderson, 1977, p. 6).

There is more to the 'strange history' than even this. As Piccone (1976, p. 488) observes, after the production of his texts,

> What happened to Gramsci closely parallels what happened to Marx after his death when Engels, in further elaborating and popularizing his thought, defused it of most of its relevant features, positivized the dialectic, and generally paved the way for the Marxisms of the Second International. In Togliatti, Gramsci found his Engels.

Togliatti, a close friend of Gramsci's, survived him to become the leader of the Italian Communist Party, and its chief theoretician. As such, he incorporated Gramsci into post-war Italian Communism as a Marxist theorist who provided a 'brilliant theoretical footnote' (Piccone, 1976, p. 489) to Lenin, a Lenin interpreted within the framework of Stalinist direction and social democratic policies.[1] Given all this, it is not surprising that Anderson (1977, p. 6) observes that the 'reconstruction of the hidden order within these hieroglyphs remains to be done,' particularly with reference to the concept of 'hegemony'. It is to this task that commentators such as Femia (1975), Merrington (1972), Sallach (1974), Salamini (1974; 1975), Williams (1960), Boggs (1976) and, most significantly, Anderson (1977) have addressed themselves.

Hegemony: the context of its development

Anderson (1977, p. 15) informs us that the term *gegemoniya* (hegemony) was widely used in the context of the Russian social democratic movement from the late 1890s to 1917, as a strategic theoretical term signalling the necessity for the proletariat to develop a commanding class consciousness in the political struggle. After the socialist revolution of 1917, the concept 'fell into relative disuse in the Bolshevik Party . . . it was rendered inoperative' by the direct transition to the dictatorship of the proletariat. The usage of hegemony in the context of the proletariat gaining ideological ascendancy over the peasantry and semi-proletariat, in order to defeat the bourgeoisie, became redundant once it seemed that this objective had been achieved.

Anderson (p. 18) records how the term 'hegemony', despite its relative demise within Russia after 1917, remained in use in the external documents of the Communist International, so that by 1922 the term was used in the context of obstacles to socialism, in those situations where the bourgeoisie maintained a political ascendancy over the proletariat, by inducing the latter to adopt a bourgeois world-view. Gramsci, as a participant at the Fourth World Congress of the Communist International became directly acquainted with the idea of hegemony in this context. What Gramsci was to achieve was the transition of the idea into a concept.

This transition is not smooth, partly for reasons already alluded to. Gramsci (1971, p. 161) begins to use the concept in *The Modern Prince* in terms of the context of the orthodox usage of the Fourth World Congress: the situation in which the proletariat struggles to gain hegemonic ascendancy. This hegemony is both an ascendancy of 'ideal' (Crocean) and 'material' (Marxian) factors: 'although hegemony is ethico-political, it must also be economic, must necessarily be based on the decisive function exercised by the leading group in the decisive nucleus of economic activity' (Gramsci, 1971, p. 161).

The transition in Gramsci's work from this orthodox use of the notion of hegemony, to the development of it as a concept for understanding bourgeois rule in a capitalist mode of production, occurs in his discussion of the 'dual perspective', 'the dialectical unity of the moments of force and consent in political action' (Hoare; in Gramsci, 1971, p. 169), a policy of the Fifth World Congress of the Communist International. The terms that he uses to discuss this 'dual perspective' are 'domination' and 'hegemony'.

His use of the concept of domination is quite specific in this instance, and is quite dissimilar to the uses which Clegg (1975) and Giddens (1976) were to develop. These later usages, which stress the 'ideological' rather than the 'coercive' aspects of domination, are much closer to Gramsci's use of hegemony. Gramsci (1971) reserves the concept of domination for more direct, physical coercion. This concept of domination is tied quite specifically to the coercive exercise of power, in a manner analogous to the relation in Weber (1968; see Clegg, 1975, pp. 56–66) of legitimate domination and power.

Gramsci (1971, p. 57) argues that before domination, as a coercive exercise of power, can be legitimate, the group exercising it must already have *direzione* (leadership). This leadership, to be 'effective', 'should not count only on the material force which power gives' (p. 59). To be effective, the '"normal" exercise of hegemony . . . is characterized by the combination of force and consent' (p. 80). To consider either apart from the other would be to sunder the dialectical unity of the 'dual perspective', which

> can present itself on various levels, from the most elementary to the
> most complex; but these can all theoretically be reduced to two
> fundamental levels. . . . They are the levels of force and of consent,
> authority and hegemony, violence and civilization, of the individual
> moment and of the universal moment . . . of agitation and of
> propaganda, of tactics and of strategy (Gramsci, 1971, pp. 169–70).

Gramsci (1971, p. 12) locates 'domination' and 'direction' not only as elements in the 'dual perspective' but also as differential locations within the social formation, in respectively 'State' and 'Civil Society'. The functions of the State are to police the economy and the dominant mode of production through a coercive, or what Althusser (1971) was to call repressive, State apparatus. Civil Society is the domain of 'so-called private organizations' through which a social group exercises ideological direction. This account of the 'dialectical unity', with each element given a specific site and function within the social formation, is the 'predominant' one in the *Notebooks*, as Anderson (1977, p. 25) remarks.[2]

Anderson observes that, while hegemony is a primary function of 'private organizations' and force a primary function of the State, hegemony enters into the equation twice, in a way in which ordinarily coercion does not. The State, in Weber's (1948, p. 78) terms, is the institution which employs a monopoly of legitimate violence over a given territory, a capacity which is 'juridically absent from civil society' (Anderson, 1977, p. 32), except in those areas and cases where the hegemonic functioning of the State fails (e.g., see McCullough and Shannon, 1977) and State functions pass to non-juridical agencies. It is Gramsci's 'conceptual slippage' on the 'key distribution' of the 'asymmetry between civil society and the State in the West: coercion is located in the one, consent in both' which poses, for Anderson (p. 41), a crucial problem: 'Beyond their distribution, what is the *inter-relation* or *connection* between consent and coercion in the structure of bourgeois class power in metropolitan capitalism . . . within Gramsci's framework everything depends on an accurate calibration of precisely this relation. How should it be conceived, theoretically?'

It is to an attempt to answer this question that we will turn next. This preliminary analysis is born out of a mediation between an earlier attempt to answer these questions within the context of 'organizations' (Clegg, 1975) and the present reflections.

Hegemonic domination and the structure of power

It is time to elaborate more fully what hegemony is, and is not, and how, as consent, it can be conceived in relation to domination as coercion.

Williams (1960, p. 587), one of the earliest English-speaking commentators on Gramsci's work, formulates the concept, 'in the most general terms', as

> a 'moment', in which the philosophy and practice of a society fuse or are in equilibrium; an order in which a certain way of life and thought is diffused throughout society in all its institutional and private manifestations, informing with its spirit all taste, morality, customs, religions and political principles, and all social relations, particularly in their intellectual and moral connotation

and observes that Gramsci 'explicitly states' that hegemony is the '"normal" form of control', and that 'force and coercion' only become 'dominant' 'at times of crisis' (Williams, 1960, p. 591)[3]. Femia (1975, p. 31) regards hegemony in Gramsci similarly as 'the predominance obtained by consent rather than force of one class or group over other classes . . . attained through the myriad ways in which the institutions of civil society . . . shape, directly and indirectly, the cognitive and affective structures whereby men perceive and evaluate problematic social reality'. Femia, in an echo of Bachrach and Baratz (1962), says that 'Gramsci eventually came to view hegemony as the most important *face* of power' (Femia, 1975, p. 31; my emphasis).

Merrington (1972, p. 152) develops the relationship between power and hegemony further, noting that

> The concept of hegemony is thus linked to Gramsci's aim to re-define the nature of power in modern societies in more comprehensive terms, allowing for the articulations of the various levels or instances of a given social formation, political, cultural or ideological, in the determination of a specific power structure.

In a letter to his sister-in-law, Tatiana, dated 7 September, 1931, Gramsci explicitly connects the process whereby hegemony functions with the role of 'the intellectuals'. His letter outlines some proposed research concerning the concept of the State conceived as

> a balance between political society and civil society, by which I mean the hegemony of one social group over the entire nation, exercised through so-called private organizations like the Church, trade unions, or schools. For it is above all in civil society that intellectuals exert their influence (Gramsci, 1975, p. 204).

Intellectuals are formed out of and reflect back upon 'the original terrain of an essential function in the world of economic production' (Gramsci, 1971, p. 5) inhabited, historically, by distinct social groups each of which creates, as well as itself, 'organically, one or more strata of intellectuals which give it homogeneity and an awareness of its own function not only in the economic but also in the social and political fields' (Gramsci, 1971, p. 5). Gramsci cites as an example of such a social group the process whereby the 'capitalist entrepreneur creates alongside himself the industrial technician, the specialist in political economy, the organizers of a new culture, of a new legal system, etc.' (ibid.). An élite amongst these entrepreneurs

> must have the capacity to be an organizer of society in general, including all its complex organism of services, right up to the State organism, because of the need to create the conditions most favourable to the expansion of their own class; or at the least they must possess the capacity to choose the deputies (specialized employees) to whom to entrust this activity of organizing the general system of relationships external to the business itself. It can be observed that the 'organic' intellectuals which every new class

creates alongside itself and elaborates in the course of its
development, are for the most part 'specializations' of partial
aspects of the primitive activity of the new social type which the new
class has brought into prominence (Gramsci, 1971, pp. 5–6).

The intellectuals thus have a crucial role in Gramsci's thought,
because they are the custodians of 'the sphere of ideology' by which
means 'consciousness is mediated in capitalist society, preserved
and protected behind the whole complex of institutions, private
and public, which legitimize bourgeois dominance, rendering its
values and definitions universal because accepted as the definitive
values of society as such' (Merrington, 1972, p. 154). When this
situation exists, there is an equilibrium between 'leadership' or
'direction' based on consent and 'domination' (*dominazione*)
which is based on coercion. Gramsci characterizes this as an
'historical bloc', the situation of class hegemony, mediated by the
intellectuals as agents promoting ideological and political unity, a
unity which universalizes a particular class rule.

The achievement of hegemonic functioning through an historical
bloc becomes the normal mode of the functioning of power. It is
only in moments of crisis, when control, which is ordinarily
structured in and through hegemony, slips or fails, that power has
to be directly exercised in order to attempt to restore this control.
Such an exercise of power signals not the presence of a strong
'capacity' for power, but instead indicates that this exercise of
power flows from a position of weakness. This position is one in
which hegemony has failed and so power is exerted in an attempt to
reassert the 'normal' situation of control.

The absence of the exercise of power does not mean the absence
of power. It signals the presence of a far more subtle and powerful
power—the power of a capacity for any further action. Anderson
(1977, p. 43) expresses this clearly with respect to the political
system:

> In the political system, a . . . structural (non-additive and
> non-transitive) relationship between ideology and repression,
> consent and coercion, prevails. The normal conditions of ideological
> subordination of the masses—the day to day routines of a
> parliamentary democracy—are themselves *constituted* by a silent,
> absent force which gives them their currency: the monopoly of
> legitimate violence by the State. Deprived of this, the system of
> cultural control would be instantly fragile, since the limits of
> possible actions against it would disappear. With it, it is immensely
> powerful—so powerful that it can, paradoxically, do 'without' it: in

effect, violence may normally scarcely appear within the bounds of the system at all.

In an organization the situation is similar, although complicated by the extension of civil and legal rights, such as unemployment benefit and other forms of social welfare, and by legislation restricting the right of management to directly coerce workers by withdrawing jobs from them as a specific discriminatory practice against particular individuals. This does not limit the fundamentally coercive nature of the labour-capital relationship, however, whereby labour has to sell itself to capital as the owner and controller of the means of production in order to work and thus, indirectly, to live. Nor does it limit the capacity of capital to choose not to reproduce itself in ways which are socially useful if it can re-reproduce profit more rapidly in alternative ways. And if these alternative ways involve unemployment for particular workers, perhaps through shifting investments into overseas production or non-productive property speculation, then nothing exists to prevent capital from doing this.

Much of the time the power of capital does not have to be exercised to be present. It is present in the absence of its exercise, because this exercise is grounded in a structural 'capacity' which frequently obviates the necessity of this exercise. This capacity is visible in the routine practices of everyday life. Westergaard and Resler (1975, pp. 141–277) are among the few writers on power (along with Pahl and Winkler, 1974; Parry and Morris, 1974; and Clegg, 1975) who have stressed the importance of these as 'certain social mechanisms, principles, assumptions . . . taken for granted' (Westergaard and Resler, 1975, p. 142). As they note, these typically 'favour the interests of this or that group *vis-à-vis* the rest of the population. The favoured group enjoys effective power, even when its members take no active steps to exercise power . . . simply because things work their way in any case' (pp. 142–3). No mystery surrounds these 'mechanisms and assumptions'. In a capitalist society, they are 'those, in the first instance, of private property and the market . . . which largely determine the living conditions of the people and the use of resources' (p. 143). These

> clearly favour the interests of capital: they confer power on capital in
> a very real and tangible sense. But the proof of that power is not to
> be found only, or even chiefly, in the fact that capitalists make
> decisions. It is to be found in the fact that the decision which both
> they and others—including government—make, and the sheer

87

> routine conduct of affairs even without definite decision-making, in
> the main have a common denominator: an everyday acceptance of
> private property and market mechanisms. It is taken for granted, 'in
> the way things work', that profit should be the normal yardstick of
> investment in most areas of activity: that the living standards of the
> propertyless majority should be set primarily by the terms on which
> they sell or are sold their labour. . . . The power of capital, to
> repeat, is revealed much less in positive acts of decision-making
> —involving conflict and choice between alternative policies—
> than in the everyday, for much of the time unquestioned, application
> of those assumptions which give priority to private capital
> accumulation and market exchange in the use and distribution
> of resources. *Power is to be found more in uneventful routine
> than in conscious and active exercise of will* (Westergaard and
> Resler, 1975, pp. 143–4; my emphasis).

Ordinarily, as Westergaard and Resler demonstrate, capital does
not maintain order in its domain through the remote threat of
coercion. It has no need to most of the time. In order to understand
this, Gramsci's work is important for any analysis of power in
organizations.

Gramsci's focus is on the role of superstructural elements in the
dense social formations of the capitalist West. These have become
sufficiently institutionalized that, even in moments of severe
structural crisis in the economic sphere, such are the opacity and
unyieldingness of a people's ordinarily available ways of theorizing
(for instance, in the media: see, Glasgow Media Collective, 1976;
McQueen, 1977), that the consequences of crises in the economic
system remain more or less taken for granted. Little effort is
expended in critique or counter-strategy, because the weapons of
critique are not available. Unemployment, inflation, or wage cuts
can come to be accepted as normal, as natural, as something which
could not have been otherwise, as their sense is constituted in and
through hegemonic forms of theorizing. One could cite examples of
the Callaghan-led British Labour Government's execution of, and
incorporation of Labour into, policies dictated by those
monetarist theorists of capital who are entombed in the various
international institutions of the world capitalist system, such as the
International Monetary Fund, the World Bank, and so on. Such
theorizing as their economic domination dictates is made to appear
as if it were the only possible, and hence natural, way of acting,
from which routine practices and outcomes flow unquestionably.

The dominant institutional domain and hegemony of the

ideological apparatus at a particular moment becomes regarded as the 'universal moment', the 'organizing principle' (in the phrase of Habermas, 1976) of our being and time as it permeates throughout civil society. Any concrete social formation does not contain just one hegemony, but many, although we can point to the dominance of a particular form at different historical moments. For instance, Catholicism or Protestantism may each have had a hegemonic function in society whose importance has receded, but which still retains a specific effectivity (e.g. in Ulster) in the face of new forms of technocratic rationality. The concept of hegemony is thus not necessarily tied to class, as was the strictly Marxist concept of ideology, although one would expect that the dominant hegemony would be. The formal domination of a world-view expressed in and through the concept of hegemony could act in ways that cut across class lines. Despite this relative autonomy, I will maintain that the relation of hegemony to a mode of production must be of particular interest.

Hegemonic domination and mode of production

A mode of production, as a concept, is an abstraction from the reality of a concrete process, and as such should not itself be the basis of any comparative analysis, but should serve only as an instrument in such an analysis. It renders an account of a particular historically distinctive combination of productive forces and relationships of production. Those are

> all the factors of production, including resources, equipment and men, which are to be found in a specific society at a specific time, and which must be combined in a specific way to produce the material goods which the society needs. The notion of relationships of production covers the functions fulfilled by individuals and groups in the process of production and in the control of the factors of production (Godelier, 1970, p. 341).

The capitalist mode of production signifies

> the relationships between a class of individuals who possess as their own private property the productive forces and the capital, and a class of individuals who possess neither of these and who must sell to the former class the use of their labour in exchange for a wage. Each class is complementary to the other and presupposes the other (Godelier, 1970, p. 341).

89

Marx argues that a mode of production is ultimately made specific by the economy. This is composed of material factors which are invariant elements (labourers, non-labourers and means of production) capable of combination in any number of ways. The 'ideal' factors of this combination concern a two-fold relation of the invariant elements: the relation between the labourer and the means of production; the relation between non-labourers and the product of the first relationship. As Poulantzas (1973, p. 27) puts it:

> The determination of a mode of production by the economic in the last instance, and of the articulation and index of dominance of its instances depends precisely on the forms which the combination in question takes on.

What are the other elements of social practice in addition to the economic? Althusser (1969, p. 167) would answer that they were, in addition, political, ideological and theoretical. Now, it is possible to separate these out analytically and apportion them, or sub-divide them, within the context of any particular social formation. Additionally, it is possible to analyse them in their interdependency and contradiction within a specific region and any given complex structured whole.

Within the 'complex whole' of society, as Althusser (1969, p. 205) argues, 'the "relations of production" are not the pure phenomena of the forces of production; they are also the conditions of its existence. The superstructure is not the pure phenomenon of the structure, it is also its condition of existence.' Taken together with a more recent work of Althusser on the reproduction of the conditions of production (1971), this mode of thinking about the 'superstructure' will lead us to a conceptualization of 'hegemony' which, when theorized as a reflexive moment of the mode of (re)-production, *in specific instances*, can illuminate the concept of domination as an element of the structural, political, ideological and theoretical functioning of material life.

Althusser broaches these issues:

> It is not enough to ensure for labour power the material conditions of its reproduction if it is to be reproduced as labour power . . . the available labour power must be 'competent', i.e. suitable to be set to work in the complex system of the process of production. . . . The reproduction of labour power requires not only a reproduction of its skills, but also, at the same time, a reproduction of its submission to the rules of the established order, i.e. a reproduction of

submission to the ruling ideology for the workers, and a reproduction of the ability to manipulate the ruling ideology correctly for the agents of exploitation and repression, so that they too will provide for the domination of the ruling class 'in words'. . . . The reproduction of labour power thus reveals as its *sine qua non* not only the reproduction of its 'skills' but also the reproduction of its subjection to the ruling ideology or of the 'practice' of that ideology, with the proviso that it is not enough to say 'not only but also', for it is clear that *it is in the forms and under the forms of ideological subjection that provision is made for the reproduction of the skills of labour power* (Althusser, 1971, pp. 126; 127–8).

Althusser calls these forms the *Ideological State Apparatus* and contrasts this form of *subjection* with that which functions through the *Repressive State Apparatus*. The contrast is between functioning primarily through 'ideology' or through 'violence', which is institutionally located, for example, in the family or the police. Unfortunately, apart from his brief allusion in the previous citations, he nowhere discusses the role and functioning of ideology in the institutional area of *specifically capitalist* institutions: that is, the production and reproduction of material life through capitalism's organizational functioning. The difficulty of doing so is of course due to Althusser's appending the ideological apparatus as a necessary part of the state. While evident links exist between state and industry at the empirical level (e.g., see Martin, 1977, ch. 10, for a convenient summary), and one can argue whether, theoretically, the state in capitalist society is a capitalist state or not (see the Poulantzas–Milliband debate in Urry and Wakeford, 1973), it would seem, as Milliband (1969, p. 59) argues, that

> To suggest that the relevant institutions are actually part of the State System does not seem to me to accord with reality, and tends to obscure the difference in this respect between these political systems and systems where ideological institutions are indeed part of a State monopolistic system of power. In the former systems, ideological institutions do retain a very high degree of autonomy; and are therefore the better able to conceal the degree to which they do not belong to the system of capitalist power.

With this in mind, let us refer only to ideological apparatus, rather than State Ideological Apparatus. We can conceive of this as having several more or less distinct institutional areas: the family, education, the economy and so on. Within, and cutting across, these different and distinct institutional areas will be numerous organizations. These organizations, as alluded to in chapter 1, have become the 'real object' of an autonomous discipline, the administrative science of organization theory.

On the surface, nearly all organizations, whether they be oriented towards the appropriation of private profit or public good, would appear to be similar. So it has appeared to the majority of organization theorists and sociologists who have succeeded Weber (1947) in their analyses of bureaucracy (e.g., Eisenstadt, 1959; Blau, 1955; Udy, 1959).

One of the few sociologists to have explicitly questioned these ontological assumptions is Herbert Marcuse (1971). One way of formulating the debate that Marcuse engaged with Weber's texts would be to pose the following question: Does the idea of Reason contained in Weber's ideal type of bureaucracy have its grounding in a universal value of bureaucracy or in a historically bounded value of capitalism?

Clearly, as Hobsbawm (1975, pp. 216–17) shows, and as Weber (1948, p. 261) stated, 'No special proof is necessary to show that military discipline is the ideal model for the modern capitalist factory.' In its origins, neither 'the autocracy of the family nor the small-scale operation of craft industry and merchant business provided much guidance for the really large capitalist organization' (Hobsbawm, 1975, p. 216). The example of the most developed forms of bureaucracy, the theory of which Weber found in, and developed from, the Prussian military forces, and which enterprises such as the British railway companies actually took over from the rank system of the British Army, was to become the specific form of management of big business:

> Today it is primarily the capitalist market economy which demands that the official business of the administration be discharged precisely, unambiguously, continuously, and with as much speed as possible. Normally, the very large, modern capitalist enterprises are themselves unequalled models of strict bureaucratic organization. Business management throughout rests on increasing precision, steadiness, and above all, the speed of operations. . . .
> Bureaucratization offers above all the optimum possibility for carrying through the principle of specializing administrative functions according to purely objective considerations. . . . . The 'objective' discharge of business primarily means a discharge of business according to calculable rules and 'without regard for persons' (Weber, 1947, p. 215).

As Marcuse (1971, p. 136) observes, 'the main basis of this

rationality is abstraction . . . the reduction of *quality* to *quantity*'. The qualities of the person are disregarded in favour of their quantification as factors of production having a specific value. The bureaucracy is built up on this basis—it is materially supported by virtue of the specific value accruing from the appropriation of labour power. This appropriation may be immediate, where the bureaucracy is supported within a profit-oriented enterprise on the basis of deductions from that enterprise's surplus value, or it may be mediated, the primary mediator in contemporary capitalist society being the State.

The 'service' that bureaucracy provides has to be seen analytically as the service of the irrational ideal of profitability whose rule and domination provide the 'framework of the calculable chances of gain in private enterprise, i.e. in the context of the *profit* of the individual entrepreneur or enterprise' (Marcuse, 1971, p. 136). What service is provided, and who is serviced, depends upon the employer's calculation of the gain in value likely to accrue from their employment as formally free quantities of labour. As Schroyer (1972, p. 114) notes: 'What Weber would call "rationalization" can now be seen as a special type of rationalization—that which can increase value production.' As such, it may be said to have a 'hegemonic functioning' (also see Cohen, 1972).

This rationalization is that which is operative and functioning in and through the everyday routines and rule of production. It is because of this constant reconstitution and reproduction of the routine in, through and by production and the practices that are production—from the most 'authoritative' executive action to the most habitual reflex of the production worker—that the mode of production is 'directly encountered, given and transmitted from the past' and re-made in the present.

In any work situation the people engaged in that work will usually be encountered doing more than just 'that work'. Another way of putting this would be to say that the hegemony of 'work' is not absolute. Normal work frequently includes practices of sabotage, theft, cultural discussion, politics and a myriad other aspects of life. In this way one may point to elements of religious, cultural or political hegemony in any specific work setting.

If one were to focus empirically on any particular work settings, then, with regard to these, one could analytically concentrate on any of a number of coterminous hegemonic elements. Not all hegemonic practice will be 'equivalent'. Within the business organization of the modern firm, for instance, one can quite clearly relate the enterprise's hegemonic functioning to its material functioning within the content of the capitalist mode of production. While labour, as the primary and determinant practice within any mode of production, is the source of material transformation, the continued possibilities of the reproduction of this practice in an evolving sense (in terms of its contradictions and order) will require the 'objective principle' of a particular hegemony in dominance. Hence, we may speak of patterns of hegemonic dominance and subordination within the specific practices of work in the organization at any one time and space.

In some instances, there exists a reflexive reciprocity between the mode of production and hegemonic dominance. Here, the 'linguistic labour' of hegemony will be a reflexive feature of the reproduction of the setting. In this case, the hegemony will 'reproduce the conditions of production at the same time as it [is] produced' (Althusser, 1971, p. 123).

It is on such occasions as this, when the theorizing power of hegemony reflexively reconstitutes the mode of production of its own practice, independently of the conscious knowledge of particular agents engaged in production, that I believe we may refer (in the sense of Clegg, 1975) to the concept of a 'form of life'. This is the ground of specific human practices exhibited in the unity of a mode of production reflexively reproduced through the hegemonic dominance of unreflected, reified convention. It should be quite clear that this may refer to theoretical, just as much as material, production and practice. In either case, the production of material or ideal artefacts, it is, in Gramsci's phrase, 'the intellectuals' who produce and reproduce the raw material of hegemony.

These intellectuals are distinctly related to particular institutional domains of the ideological apparatus, with a particular domain being dominant at different moments in the development of a mode of production in different social formations. Gramsci (1971, p. 285) observes, for instance, that one reason for twentieth-century American capital's ascendancy is that it does not have the leaden burden of 'great historical and cultural traditions' to support. It is because

> these preliminary conditions existed, already rendered rational by historical evolution, (that) it was relatively easy to rationalize production and labour by a skilful combination of force (destruction of working class trade unionism on a territorial basis) and persuasion (high wages, various social benefits, extremely subtle

ideological and political propaganda) and thus succeed in making
the whole life of the Nation revolve around production. *Hegemony
here is born in the factory and requires for its exercise only a minute
quantity of professional political and ideological intermediaries*
(Gramsci, 1971, p. 285; my emphasis).

Hegemony in the factory is born out of specific practices devised
by the intellectual cadre of the factory and mediated by
management. This cadre is that of the administrative and
organization sciences.

Analysis of power in factory organizations needs to begin by
specifying both those practices and the intellectual production of
them which maintain hegemony as the 'normal' functioning of a
situation, for it is in these instances, rather than those of 'crisis',
that power is least visible. In just such instances of hegemony, then,
analysis of power in organizations constituted under the
knowledge-interest of that hegemony can fulfil a decisive function.
It can appear to discuss power in the situation, which seemingly
ought to render that situation transparent, but which in fact serves
only to make its social reality more opaque. Thus, it acts not only
as a further agency of hegemony, but also as the most potentially
effective, because it blunts the concepts of critical analysis.

The following chapter addresses these issues, and in so doing
provides both one instance of the critical practice that this text is
attempting to develop and a microcosmic application of the
structure of the argument in all the preceding pages.

This discussion can now be reformulated in terms of the model
which I originally proposed in *Power, Rule and Domination*
(1975), but which I have simplified by substituting Giddens' (1976,
p. 122) use of the conceptual distinctions of action, mediation and
structure for my earlier distinctions of surface structure, deep
structure and form of life. At the levels of action, mediation and
structure, respectively, I will define the concepts of power, rule and
hegemonic domination.

1 Power

We will observe that, historically, power in organizations has
consisted of the ability to control means and methods of
production. More abstractly and generally, we can say that power
is the ability to exercise control over resources which, when subjects
engage in practices, produce effects on other subjects. In this
instance, the practice that we are concerned with is that practice

which is the visible structure of social relations in the organization, and changes in these relations.

2 Rule

Individual power practices, when treated collectively as discrete events within the totality of the organization, may be analytically constituted as displaying an underlying *rule*. This rule is expressed through the formulation of 'deep sameness' in phenomenologically 'surface difference', in terms of the underlying *mode of rationality* of the production of the phenomena of the surface of social life by subjects. The mode of rationality is analysed as a property of structures, not of subjects. It is the analytic ground of the expression of particular subjectivities in and through labour. It is a formal, abstract concept. In *Power, Rule and Domination*, the rule of a mode of rationality was analysed substantively in terms of the strategies which the members of a construction site employed in their daily routine of negotiation, in particular in the context of site meetings. These strategies consisted of attempting to formulate the inherently indexical contractual documents which constituted the site in terms of their own organizationally defined interests (e.g. Project Manager versus Clerk of Works, or Chief Architect).

In this work, the concept of mode of rationality will be applied not to substantive empirical instances, but to the construction of an abstract historical process composed of different forms of organizational intervention in the sphere of production (the labour process) and the sphere of distribution (the market). It will be argued that both historically and analytically, the sphere of production is the initial point of departure.

What the next chapter does is to construct an abstract, formal model of an historically possible mode of rationality within the capitalist mode of production. It is designed to define a particular structure of economic social relations, the organization. This may then be of use in the analysis of specific organization structures.

The concept of organization *structure* used here is developed from Offe (1972), who conceives of 'structure' as a set of sedimented (i.e. historically laid down and superimposed) selection rules. These sedimented selection rules constitute those phenomena that the structure attends to as matters requiring regulation—what we may term its 'enacted environment' (after Weick, 1969). Habermas (1976, p. 60) defines these sedimented selection rules, which can be conceptualized as structure, as determining 'what is thematized, what—with what priority and by which means—is actually publicly regulated, etc. The relatively stable administrative patterns of helping and hindering are objectively functional for capital realization, that is, they are independent of the professed intentions of the administration. They can be explained with the aid of selection rules that predetermine the consideration or suppression of problems, themes, arguments and interests.'

To recapitulate the argument: the mode of rationality is an abstract formal model. It defines a possible structure within a particular structure of economic social relations. This is the organization-structure. The organization-structure can be conceptualized as a structure of sedimented selection rules. These prescribe the limits within which the organization-structure might vary. Hence, the mode of rationality is not a mode of a specific organization, but an abstraction which may be used to analyse specific organization structures.

3 Hegemonic domination

The abstraction, mode of rationality, is itself conceptualized within the abstraction of the mode of production. The mode of rationality is the analytical formulation of sedimented selection rules. These rules are the means by which owners and controllers of the means of production orient their practice towards the hegemonic domination of some 'objective principle', which, in the last instance, will tend to be conditioned economically by the mode of production.[4] When we are dealing with institutional spheres constituted in the immediate production of surplus-value, the mode of production and hegemonic domination have, in the long run, a *necessary reflexive relationship* between them, existing as what I have elsewhere referred to as the *iconic domination* of a form of life (Clegg, 1975). More simply, we could say that this relationship provides the *ground rules* of the mode of production. These have been specified, originally by Karl Marx, for the capitalist mode of production, and most rigorously by Hindess and Hirst (1975, p. 10):

> Capitalist relations of production define a mode of appropriation of surplus-labour which works by means of commodity exchange. Capitalists buy means of production and items of personal consumption from each other. They buy labour-power from labourers in exchange for wages. With these wages the labourers buy items of personal consumption from capitalists and must then sell their labour-power for a further period in order to be able to buy further means of personal consumption. Appropriation of

surplus-labour here depends on a difference between the value of labour-power and the value that may be created by means of the labour-power. Surplus-labour takes the form of surplus-value. This appropriation of surplus-labour presupposes that means of production are in the hands of the capitalists, since otherwise there is no necessity for the labourers to obtain means of consumption through the sale of their labour-power. Thus capitalist relations of production define a mode of appropriation of surplus-labour in the form of surplus-value, and a social distribution of the means of production so that these are the property of non-labourers (capitalists), while the labour-power takes the form of a commodity which members of the class of labourers are forced to sell to members of the class of non-labourers.

To elaborate, Marx (1973b) argues that what the worker sells to the capitalist in return for his wages is his labour power. Marx maintains that this cannot be a fair exchange. If it were, the capitalist would quickly have no money left, because, if the capitalist did not share in the labour, then all the money would soon pass to the labourer. Where there existed profit there could be no fair exchange. What might appear on the surface to be a just exchange 'inducing' the 'contribution' of organizational membership will in fact have to be an unjust and exploitative exchange if the organization as the capitalist's instrument for materializing profit is to remain in being in the long run. In capitalist organizations exploitation is the material basis of capital's domination of labour as a class (as Cole's introduction to Marx, 1974, reiterates concisely). Capital, and its functionaries in management—between whom Marx (1962, p. 427) argues that no distinction be made—has a greater prior capacity for an exercise of power because its very existence is premised on the diminution of the power of labour (also see Macpherson, 1973, pp. 43–5).

In spheres other than those concerned with the institutional area of the economy, the level of domination is only contingently determined by the mode of production. This allows subjects considerably more choice, theoretically, at the surface level of social practice and action. None the less, this freedom, as all freedom, is conditioned, and one can hypothesize rules which condition the selection of strategies of action. We can represent the model diagrammatically, as Figure 2.

Figure 2 The mode of rationality of the development of the organization structure

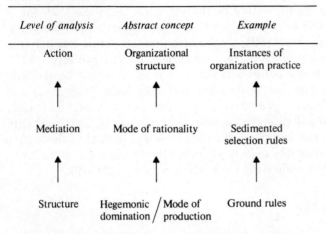

Level of analysis	Abstract concept	Example
Action	Organizational structure	Instances of organization practice
↑	↑	↑
Mediation	Mode of rationality	Sedimented selection rules
↑	↑	↑
Structure	Hegemonic domination / Mode of production	Ground rules

The model is not static. In addition to being an analysis of structures, it is necessarily an analysis of structures through time, with a time-lagged function. This may also be represented diagrammatically, in Figure 3.

Figure 3 Time and structure

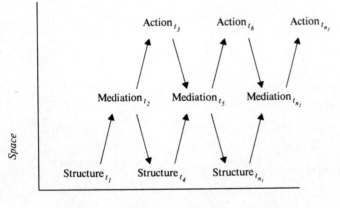

The distinctions in 'space' in Figure 3 are located in an analytical sense of space as 'structure' rather than space as descriptive co-ordinate. Thus, the present moment of action (t_3) is always produced from a past moment of structural conjuncture (t_1)

99

mediated through strategies located at moment (t_2), yet it is used to refer to a mediation (t_5) which is in the future, and so on. Depending on the nature of the empirical materials that one is detailing, this will involve research whose temporal unfolding is at the level of surface (this was the case with my earlier research into the structuring of action on a construction site (see Clegg, 1975), from which one constitutes the structure. This will be the case where one can observe the constitution of action in practice and process. Where one is dealing with the history of already constituted and embodied action, then one will be concerned with the level of mediation, at which level one will attempt to analyse the mode of rationality of that which is already unfolded, in terms of the strategies underlying the practice which produced it.[5]

Chapter 7
Power, control, structure and organization

Power in organization theory

If one knew nothing of organizations in contemporary society, yet was willing to absorb what knowledge one could from existing scholarly texts on the topic, what picture of power would these present? One would find that the development of a specific concern with 'power' in the theory of organizations is related to the post-Hawthorne 'discovery' of the informal organization (Roethlisberger and Dickson, 1939; Landsberger, 1958). Prior to this the usual focus of enquiry was the structure of formal authority, as Thompson (1956, p. 290) suggests:

> The usual definitions of power are properly applicable to the internal structures of formal organizations. One reason why research workers have seldom regarded actual power in such organizations may be that the classics on bureaucracy have stressed the rational aspects of organization, with emphasis on authority to the neglect of unauthorized or illegitimate power. And it was not long ago that informal organization was 'discovered' in bureaucracies.

Thompson indicts the 'classics of bureaucracy' for their neglect of 'power' to the benefit of 'authority'. As Weber's work represents the essential 'classics of bureaucracy' for most sociologists, one might think that Weber is responsible for the neglect of 'power' in organization theory. Except that Weber is so frequently cited as the source of a concern with 'power'. This seeming anomaly is explicable when one considers the context in which Weber's 'classics of bureaucracy' were translated and incorporated into American sociology.

Weber's work on 'power' and 'authority' became available to most organization theorists through Parsons and Henderson's translation known as *The Theory of Social and Economic Organization* (Weber, 1947). In a much-remarked-upon footnote by Parsons (Weber, 1947, p. 152), the concept of *Herrschaft* is translated as 'authority', thus preserving what Gouldner (1970) has called Parsons' 'superordinate' view of power, as if it were

Weber's. This 'superordinate' concept leads Parsons to regard 'power' and 'authority' in two ways:

> either as two different stages in development, in which, for instance, power is viewed as the degenerate or the immature form of authority; or as two alternative ways in which one person or group can structure the behaviour of others. In both cases they are viewed as mutually exclusive, as if, when one exists, the other does not. . . . If it had been looked at from the standpoint of *subordination* in the social world, power and authority would more likely be viewed as dual structures, both *simultaneously* present, in subtle and continual interaction. Power, in short, exists not simply when authority breaks down, or before authority has had a chance to mature. It exists as a factor in the lives of subordinates, shaping their behaviour and beliefs, at every moment of their relations with those above them. . . . Legitimacy and 'authority' never eliminate power; they merely defocalize it, make it latent (Gouldner, 1970, p. 294).

In those studies which have followed Parsons' 'view' of 'power' as a 'superordinate' concept, then 'power' relates to 'authority' as something distinct, as something 'informally' rather than 'formally' developed. This becomes the theme for the development of organization theory studies of power. For instance, Bennis *et al.* (1958) follow this view in noting the 'formal-informal' distinction as one in which 'authority is the *potentiality* to influence based on a position, whereas power is the actual ability of influence based on a number of factors, including of course, organizational position' (Bennis *et al.*, 1958, p. 144).

This definition of the topic becomes the basis for the mainstream of organization theory studies of power. The focus of investigation is defined in terms of deviations from the formal structure. This formal structure then appears in the analysis only in so far as it frames the initial state of rest, of equilibrium, from which the power deviation is to be measured. In itself it is not a topic for investigation or explanation. The topic becomes the *exercise* of power from within an initial equilibrium position, where that exercise is premised on the possession of some resource(s) by the power-holder.

Defining the topic in this way has at least two important consequences. First, it can lead to analyses of power which take the formal structure too much for granted in their zest to explicate the causal bases of power, as for instance in the recent works of Mechanic (1962) and Hickson *et al.* (1971).

Mechanic (1962) proceeds from Weber's (1952) argument that

permanent officials can frequently exercise power over elected representatives because such officials have a special knowledge due to their permanency *vis-à-vis* members elected for the life of a parliament. He then extends this argument to all organizations. It is hardly legitimate to extend an argument concerned with representative government to all organizations in general. It is certainly not legitimate to do so where the critical feature of the original argument is missing. This is the case where the executive is not elected on a precarious and revocable basis, compared with a permanent administrative staff.

Mechanic also displays another representative tendency in studies of 'power' which define it as the *exercise* of 'will' (Weber, 1947), 'force' (Mechanic, 1962) or 'determination' (Thompson, 1956), or any similar formulation. The tendency is to premise this 'exercise' on specific 'bases'. These 'bases' have typically been conceptualized as foundations of power, in one or other of two ways. One of these can be characterized as 'functionalist' because the bases are sought in the 'functions' of the organizational system. Examples can be seen in the work of Thompson (1956) and Dubin (1957).

In a study of two USAF bomber wings Thompson (1956) argues that these 'bases' develop 'because of the technical requirements of operations' and suggests that they include being in a 'centralized' position within the organization and being involved in strategic 'communication'. Dubin similarly stresses 'the technical requirements of operations', with his emphasis on a 'system of functional interdependence' in which some tasks will be highly 'essential' to the system and are the 'exclusive' function of a specific 'party' (Dubin, 1957, p. 62).

Bases of 'power' have also been sought in specific socially sanctioned 'resources' which the individual may control, or be in some special relationship with, so that they somehow enable 'power' to be 'exercised'. A typical formulation would be that of French and Raven (1959), in which an *a priori* list of 'power resources' is constituted. The problems with any such list, no matter what its constitution may be, are apparent. Such an explanation, if it is to be comparative, assumes that the particular 'resources' which have utility in one situation will have that utility in all situations. It also assumes perfect knowledge on the part of all people in being able to correctly judge the utility of all resources in all situations. Such assumptions are without warrant, and can only be guaranteed within the ideological practice of capitalist society, as Sensat and Constantine (1975) argue in their 'Critique of the foundations of utility theory'. Thus, explanations premised on this assumption presume that the individual utilities of different 'resources' can be aggregated on a single measuring scale. This is to deny changing historical circumstances or different societal locales. The assumption of 'resource'-based explanations of 'power' ought also to entail an exposition of how some people come to have access to these 'resources' while others do not. The prior possession of resources in anything other than equal amounts is something which a theory of 'power' has to explain. It may presume equilibrium, but it ought to justify its presumption in some way.

Organization theories of 'power' have not justified this assumption of equilibrium. They have presumed it, by the simple expedient of taking the prior and inequitable distribution of resources for granted.

This is explicable when one considers the development of the organizational theory of power from Thompson's (1956) article onwards. A 'view' of 'power in organizations' developed as a study of variance or deviance from a presumedly unproblematic formal structure. By the late 1960s there had developed a small literature on 'power in organizations'. There existed a general consensus on a concept of 'power' as an 'exercise' of 'will', 'determination', etc., which was usually modeled upon Dahl's (1957) mechanical model. The formal structure of hierarchical power in the organization was rarely discussed except in descriptive ways by writers such as Tannenbaum (1968). Increasingly, the possible 'bases' of 'power' were modelled upon abstract concepts current in the literature, rather than on specific social psychologists' lists. The most pervasive was Crozier's (1964) initially quite concrete concept of 'uncertainty', control of which he had linked to 'power' (albeit of a marginal and discretionary type). The concept was in vogue. It had become a mainstay of 'The behavioural theory of the firm' as Cyert and March (1963) modeled it. In addition, the concept of 'uncertainty' which was implicit in Thompson's (1956) stress on control of 'strategic communication' as a base of 'power' became explicit in his *Organizations in Action* (1967).

It was at this stage in the development of the language-game that a group of researchers led by Hickson attempted a 'synthesis' of much of the available material, perhaps on the basis that with a shopping list one might as well have a recipe. They called their recipe 'A strategic contingencies theory of intra-organizational power' (Hickson *et al.*, 1971).

The 'strategic contingencies' theory of power is no exception in theorizing from an initial assumption of equilibrium in the organization. The theory does not do so within the terms of the initial 'informal-formal' dichotomy. Because it is able to conceptualize the organization outside these terms it is able to abstract the formal structure of power entirely out of the analysis. Lawrence and Lorsch's (1967, p. 3) redefinition of the organization as 'a system of interrelated behaviours of people who are performing a task that has been differentiated into several distinct subsystems' provides the opportunity for this reconceptualization.

The adoption of these premises leads to a theoretical equilibrium achieved through a two-fold abstraction. First, it abstracts the prior distribution of hierarchical power out of its 'picture' through the expedient of ignoring it. The theory is able to do this by conceptualizing the organization not as pyramidal, but as an 'interdepartmental system' after the manner of Lawrence and Lorsch, in which

> the division of labour becomes the ultimate source of
> intraorganizational power, and power is explained by variables that
> are elements of each subunit's task, its functioning, and its links with
> the activities of other subunits (Hickson *et al.*, 1971, p. 217).

The second abstraction is in neglecting or not accounting for the fact that, where 'subunits' can be said to have engaged in 'the determination of behaviour' (Hickson *et al.*, 1971, p. 218), then this implies the prior power of the management of that subunit in being able to speak and act for subunit members. There is no account of how the departmental management, rather than the work force, speaks *for* the subunit, as a subunit of unitary and harmonious voices and views. The possibilities of internal conflicts and fundamental clashes of interest are never raised. That these differences count for nothing, and are rarely aired by the management of the subunit merely reaffirms the pyramidal power structure of the organization, rather than suppressing it. The 'power' of the subunit has to be grounded in the prior hierarchical *capacity* to exercise power which managers possess. This is insufficiently stressed in the literature under review, in which we find that 'power' is conceptualized as equivalent to being 'central', 'unsubstitutable', in 'control' of 'uncertainty', etc. There is no account of why a particular type of interrelationship should dispose subunits to *exercise* 'power'. Or, to de-reify the theory, why these should dispose particular managers to *exercise* 'power'. It would seem to require an implicit assumption that there exists such a craving for 'power' that anyone who has the chance to exercise it will do so.

One of the most surprising features of the previously cited literature is the way it has developed in isolation from the lively Community Power Debate in political science. One consequence of this has been the uncritical application of a concept of 'power' which has been subject to extensive criticism. I refer to the critique of Dahl's (1957) concept of 'power' by writers such as Bachrach and Baratz (1962; 1970). One writer on 'The role of "power" in organization theory', who has addressed this literature, is Abell (1975; 1976).

Abell (1975, p. 3) rejects the use of 'resources' or 'bases' as an 'operational definition' of 'power'. Instead he proposes that one should first detect the 'power' or 'influence' of a group or person and then provide an explanation of this power in terms of resources. The distinction between 'power' and 'influence' that Abell makes is quite specific, and serves the purpose of attempting to incorporate Bachrach and Baratz's (1962) critique of Dahl's concept of 'power' into organizational analysis.

The crux of Bachrach and Baratz's (1962) critique lies in the proposition that the study of 'power' should be extended to a study of 'non-decisions' as well as decisions, and to a study of the 'mobilization of bias' (Schattschneider, 1960) as it is embodied in dominant values, political myths, rituals and institutions which customarily rule in some issues while some others are just as routinely ruled out.

Abell (1975, p. 5) argues that, if we can obtain data on people's 'initial preferred outcomes' to a decision and observe 'the ability of A to modify B's preferred outcomes in a bargaining/influence situation all other influences "held constant", then this will give us the influence of A over B in securing B's "modified preferred outcomes"'. The 'bargaining power' of A will then be 'his ability to obtain his preferred outcomes, when facing competing preferred outcomes, in a bargaining situation, all other bargaining power held constant', determined by the 'final bargained outcome'. But although this approach does not simply aggregate 'bases' or 'resources' and does not depend on a simple assumption of an initial equilibrium, it is still not really satisfactory. The 'initial preferred outcomes' that people will have are, in a sense, arbitrary. They will depend upon *when* the researcher has defined the bargaining sequence as beginning. Nor is an 'initial preferred outcome' as unproblematic as it might at first sight seem to be. What constitutes an 'initial preferred outcome' may be the very problem that we wish to address, rather than its solution. To the extent that a person's theorizing of the possibilities of his existence and participation in an organization will be circumscribed within the dominant theorizing power of the organization's form of life, then surely a very significant form of power will be the members' inability to see beyond the actuality of presence? In Marcuse's (1964) phrase, they will be 'one-dimensional' people embedded within the unthought consensus of everyday life.

Through a perusal of this dominant literature (which is certainly not at all exhaustive, although it is central to ongoing research) one might be led to think that organizations were composed of 'behaviours' (Lawrence and Lorsch, 1967, p. 3) which belonged to something called a 'subunit' which occupied a space in a 'system' (Hickson *et al.*, 1971, p. 217). These subunits are engaged in a permanent struggle with each other as each tries to control more aggregated 'bases' of 'power' than the others (Butler *et al.*, 1974; Hickson *et al.*, 1971). Sometimes these behaviours and subunits form 'coalitions' with others of their kind, from inside or outside the same system. Coalitions are usually not very stable, and change over specific issues (Benson, 1975; Butler *et al.*, 1974).

As with much science fiction which features alien beings, one finds no explanation of the Hobbesian assumptions. Subunits, like Daleks, just happen to be like that. And if we recognize human beings inside the Dalek shell, or inside the subunit—well, it must just be that it is somehow *in* human nature to strive for power like that. It would seem that theoretical humanism and methodological individualism, however disguised, are at the root of power. None of our scholars tells us otherwise.

The assumption of a 'power struggle' as a principle of the system fulfils the same function in organization theory as does the principle of unfettered competition in economic models of price equilibrium (after Macpherson, 1973, pp. 184–91). These economic models are premised on the assumption of a freely competitive market for resources and commodities, in which there exists a division of labour and exchange of products and labour. It is assumed that each individual in this market would rationally try to maximize his or her gains (or minimize the real costs). Where both a division of labour and an exchange of commodities and labour exist, then it would follow that competition would determine prices for everything in a determinate system which tended to equilibrium (as Lipsey, 1963, demonstrates).

Organization theory rephrases these assumptions but without substantially altering the problematic of 'equilibrium' which they animate. In organization theory the equilibrium is achieved through the creation of 'dependencies'.

On the assumption of a power struggle in the organization's market (its 'bargaining zone' in Abell's phrase) in which, as in economic theory, each individual tried to maximize his or her gains (or minimize the real costs), where the division of labour creates exchanges, then it would follow that control of scarce 'resources' or 'bases' of exchange would maximize dependencies for everyone (as in Hickson *et al.*, 1971). And, where 'power' is defined as the obverse of 'dependency', then we would have achieved a theory of power in a determinate system which tended to equilibrium, as in economics—or in organization theory as Hickson *et al.* (1971) render it.

Such a model is premised on a market model whose motive force is a series of ontological assumptions:

> to treat the maximization of utilities as the ultimate justification of a society, is to view man as essentially a consumer of utilities. It is only when man is seen as essentially a bundle of appetites demanding satisfaction that the good society is the one which maximizes satisfactions (Macpherson, 1973, p. 4).

In distinction to this view is that which I have been elaborating in previous chapters, which stresses not only the exercise of power, but also the capacity to exercise power, as it may be limited materially or ideologically. This formulation proposes that power cannot be understood without understanding the freedom that either it is grounded in or it constrains.

It proposes an understanding of the organization as the locus of the domination of a specific form of life—that of the juncture of materials with ideas about the relationship of these to each other. These materials comprise not only the organization's site, plant, capital and raw materials, but also its labour. Within organizations constituted under a capitalist form of life, it is the case that this labour is also regarded descriptively as just another commodity to be exploited (Macpherson, 1973, p. 10). The basis of the organization is the 'labour-power' (Marx, 1973b), the 'capacity for labour' of the individuals who collectively comprise the creativity of the organization. Some of these members control not only their own creativity, their own 'capacity for labour', but also the creativity of other members through the formal distribution of domination.

Adopting this latter view has some important consequences for our theorizing. It concentrates our thought on the theoretical and practical prior conditions for the 'exercise' of 'power'. The essence of this view of 'power' is to see it as 'potential' or 'capacity' for future action, *including any specific exercise of 'power'*. In ordinary language, it would be the type of 'power' meant when we say that someone 'has power', or when we speak of someone 'being in power'.

To abstract this concept of power as capacity out of analysis is to distract our attention from the underlying social relations that grant to some positions in organizations more or less 'capacity' to 'exercise' power than to others. Instead it focuses our attention on the 'exercise' after any prior structuring of 'capacity' has occurred. 'Power' is seen simply as the 'exercise' of an 'ability', *taken after any accretion or diminution of 'capacity' has occurred*.

This concept of 'power' as a mechanical exercise does not stipulate access to whatever means are necessary to *exercise* this capacity; instead it abstracts the whole question of 'capacity' out of consideration. 'Power' is power over others only after some 'exercise' moves the state of play from some point *taken* as an initial state of rest. There is no specification of how the rules of play have developed, nor of how they might grant a greater 'capacity' to one set of players over the others. This has the ideological function of preserving the structural framework of social relations as something outside, and prior to, any theoretical enquiry into 'power'. *Thus, this structural framework cannot enter into any explanation of how the 'exercise' of power can create a 'variance' from 'authority'*.

The remainder of the argument seeks to open a space whereby this may be possible. Let us begin at the most general level.

The systems metaphor: naturalism in organizational analysis

A naturalist tendency in the analysis of organizations is most evident in the use of the concept of system. Within theories of organizations the concept of the organization as a system still remains dominant. The systems concept initially derives from cybernetic and biological sciences, where the objects of theoretical and empirical enquiry ordinarily have quite distinct 'spatial and temporal boundaries', as Habermas (1976, p. 3) puts it. In the social world the boundary problem is far more complex, and has yet to be handled satisfactorily by any organization-systems theory.

The problem of boundary determination is

> that of delimiting which objects are to be considered as parts of the system and which as parts of the environment. There does not appear to be any clear solution to this problem when patterns of human interaction are involved, because actors who are members of any particular system are themselves likely to be members of other systems and there will be interdependencies between their behaviour in all systems (Gilbert, 1972, p. 30; cited in McCullough and Shannon, 1977, p. 84).

The unsatisfactory nature of existing conceptualizations may be gauged from any 'state of the art account' (e.g. Luhmann, 1976) or textbook survey (e.g. Silverman, 1970) in which the desperate attempts of organization theorists either to keep the 'environment' out (closed systems) or else to allow it back in (open systems) have produced a variety of equally arbitrary and invariably static formulations (despite some that masquerade as 'dynamic' systems). The static nature of these models usually derives from the way the *organization-environment* relation is conceived. Within this framework, power and interaction processes are conceived as *exchange* relationships between an individual focal organization and a more or less organized, segmented or specialized environment. As Wassenberg (1977, p. 89) observes,

> This literature covers subjects such as the identification of relevant external factors with which an organization co-defines its task environments, the varying degree of consensus in these co-definitions (domain consensus) and the extension of Merton's ideas about role-sets, sanctions and rewards to organizations as role incumbents involved in exchanges of resources, prestige and compliance. With a few exceptions, however, the horizontal and equilibrium perspective predominates in these efforts. . . . Unfortunately, the basic notion of *emergence* of [power] structures from the processes of ongoing exchanges disappears completely when it is transposed from the original intraorganizational focus on socio-economic and socio-political phenomena. Exchanges between organizations become seen as the fruits of some Durkheimian division of labour, resources, and expertise in a functional framework, rather than as the consequences and cause of a *stratification* of organizations in terms of power, prestige, and resourcefulness.

110

As part of the same critique of contemporary organizational analysis, McCullough and Shannon have criticized the manner in which

> organizations can be conceived as conceptually distinct and
> removable analytically from the world around them, and it is
> accordingly on such a foundation that an examination can proceed
> of organizations, and at the same time of the organized relationships
> that may vary from one body or type of body to another in time or
> place. Hence the proliferations of studies about schools, churches,
> persons, prisons, hospitals, businesses, social welfare agencies,
> military institutions and so on (McCullough and Shannon, 1977,
> p. 73).

The only alternative to such a 'common-sense' categorization would seem to be the systems theoretic de-contextualization of the organization's specificity into a general systems model. Is it the case that either one can deal with the concrete, the particular—say, a school and a prison, but not their interrelation—or one can deal with the general, but not the specific—the 'equivocality' or 'uncertainty' of the information flow, but not the quality or content of that information? Is there no alternative?

Until recent critiques (such as, for instance, those in Clegg and Dunkerley, 1977), the organization-system-within-the-environment model has been fundamentally accepted as the premise of theories of organizations. In a world in which the 'strategic choices' (Child, 1972) available to the majority of organizations less and less control their environments, but their 'environments' control them, even up to the point of destroying the organization (the increasing rhythm of take-overs and mergers on a global scale), the paucity of this undifferentiated concept of the environment becomes more evident. *The organization*, as *a focal unit of analysis*, is increasingly *not* where the action is.

It has recently been argued by Immanuel Wallerstein (1974a; 1974b; 1976a; 1976b), in the field of comparative history, that the only sensible unit of comparative analysis for macro-sociological enquiry is the *world system*. He arrived at this position through a consideration of the question: 'What are the appropriate units to study if one . . . purports to analyse the process of social change in the modern world?' (Wallerstein, 1974a, p. 3). His difficulties in arriving at an answer to this question centred on the 'concept of stages of development' and 'criteria for determining stages, and comparability of units across historical time' (p. 6). As he puts it:

111

The crucial issue when comparing 'stages' is to determine the units
of which the 'stages' are synchronic portraits (or 'ideal types', if you
will). And the fundamental error of ahistorical social science
(including ahistorical versions of Marxism) is to reify parts of the
totality into such units and then to compare these reified structures
(Wallerstein, 1974b, p. 389).

An instance of this practice to which he refers is the acceptance
of 'society' as an empirical entity, on the assumption 'that the unit
within which social action principally occurs is a politico-cultural
unit' (Wallerstein, 1976a, p. 345), and the compounding of this
empirical fallacy by conceptualizing each unit, or society, as
characterized by a specific stage or mode, e.g. feudal, capitalist or
socialist. Such a way of thinking creates what has been a major
problem for historical analysis of post-revolutionary Russia and
China: can a stage of development be skipped? Can a society be
catapulted from a feudal to a socialist mode and bypass the
capitalist mode? Wallerstein argues that these questions are

only logically meaningful if we have 'stages' that 'co-exist' within a
single empirical framework. . . . If we are to talk of stages,
then—and we should talk of stages—it must be stages of social
systems, that is, of totalities. And the only totalities that exist or
have historically existed are mini-systems and world-systems, and in
the nineteenth and twentieth centuries there has been only one
world-system in existence, the capitalist world economy
(Wallerstein, 1974b, pp. 389–90).

What is a world economy?

As a formal structure, a world-economy is defined as a single
division of labour within which are located multiple cultures . . . but
which has no overwhelming political structure. Without a political
structure to redistribute the appropriated surplus, the surplus can
only be redistributed via the 'market', however frequently States
located within the world economy intervene to distort the market.
Hence the mode of production is capitalist (Wallerstein, 1976a, p.
348).

This concept of a capitalist world system has as a fundamental
premise the demonstration of a single division of labour which we
can regard as

a grid which is substantially interdependent. Economic actors
operate on some assumption (obviously seldom clear to any
individual actor) that the totality of their essential needs—of
sustenance, protection and pleasure—will be met over a reasonable

time-span by a combination of their own productive activities and exchange in some form. The smallest grid that would substantially meet the expectations of the overwhelming majority of actors within these boundaries constitutes a single division of labour. . . . What was happening in Europe from the sixteenth to the eighteenth centuries is that over a large geographical area going from Poland in the northeast, westwards and southwards throughout Europe and including large parts of the Western Hemisphere as well, there grew up a world-economy, for which men produced largely agricultural products for sale and profit. I would think the simplest thing to do would be to call this agricultural capitalism. . . . Capitalism was from the beginning an affair of the world-economy and not of nation-states (Wallerstein, 1974b, pp. 397, 399, 401).

The units of comparative analysis within this world economy are regional specializations occurring in specific and different areas of the world economy (Wallerstein, 1974b, p. 400).

This regional specialization comes about by the attempts of actors in the market to avoid the normal operation of the market whenever it does not maximize their profit . . . capital has never allowed its aspirations to be determined by national boundaries in a capitalist world-economy . . . thus . . . one cannot reasonably explain the strength of various state-machineries at specific moments of the history of the modern world-system primarily in terms of a genetic-cultural line of argumentation, but rather in terms of the structural role a country plays in the world economy at that moment in time (Wallerstein, 1974b, p. 403).

Within this concept of only one social system—the modern capitalist world economy—within which social change can be studied, Wallerstein (1974a, p. 7) proposes that 'sovereign states . . . be seen as one kind of organizational structure among others within this single social system'. This notion of *organizational structures within one social system* is also relevant for the general analysis of organizations. Such analysis has frequently foundered either on the epicyclical complexities (and sterility) of a modern systems theory (e.g. Weick, 1969) which sees all organizations as systems of systems within systems, without regard to problems either of boundaries or of distinctiveness in the way of the organization's functioning—the work it is designed to do, its labour—or on the microscopic retailing of the work members of organizations do in socially constructing their sense of the setting they are in, without taking account of 'the significance of interactional patterns within a structural or societal context'

(Lassman, 1974, p. 141). In addition, one can criticize both the 'cognitivist' and the 'systems' theory for their neglect of an historical perspective (e.g. see Martins', 1974, critique).

Reconceptualizing organizations in the world system

We may begin the reconceptualization of organizations as structures of regional dominance and subordination within a social system which is a world system, i.e. 'one that has boundaries, structures, member groups, rules of legitimation, and coherence', whose 'life is made up of the conflicting forces which hold it together by tension, and tear it apart as each group seeks eternally to remold it to its advantage'. Such a system 'has the characteristics of an organism in that it has a life span over which its characteristics change in some respects and remain stable in others . . . its structure . . . being at different times strong or weak in terms of the internal logic of its functioning' (Wallerstein, 1974a, p. 347). This reconceptualization would be one way of addressing what some recent critics have regarded as a key failing of organization theories, that 'they are both unhistorical and ethnocentric' (McCullough and Shannon, 1977, p. 75).

As they elaborate it:

> The point is really that all of the organizations compared and classified in different countries or regions by organizational analysts in terms of their memberships or prime beneficiaries, bases of compliance or structural characteristics, etc. may be themselves organized in relation to a nation state and to a global balance of power involving competing nations. Nations themselves may not even be the most significant organizing feature of a modern world economy. New alignments and power blocs continuously emerge and it is these which globally determine the total organization of organizations in such a way that they may be structurally connected despite the lack of apparent immediate contact required by organizational analysis. The image shifts, broadly speaking, from a sea on which ships collide or coalesce without their shockwaves extending much beyond, to a planetary constellation in which all movements are interrelated by gravitational laws (McCullough and Shannon, 1977, p. 75).

This requires elaboration. Let us begin with the concept of the organization, as it was developed by Weber (1968) in his analysis of legal-rational bureaucracy. Where the basis of the organizational power structure is of the rational-legal type, then this rationality, 'in the vast majority of cases, and indeed in the most important ones', can be seen to 'utilize . . . economic power for its foundation and maintenance' (Weber, 1968, p. 942). Such 'economic power' as a 'concrete object' is the realization of the 'objective principle' of a

> legal norm . . . established by agreement or by imposition, on grounds of expediency or value rationality or both, with a claim to obedience, [to those] . . . who stand in certain social relationships or carry out forms of social action which in the order governing the organization have been declared to be relevant (Weber, 1968; p. 217).

These social relationships are constituted through the possession of differential skills— 'technical knowledge . . . by itself, is sufficient to ensure . . . a position of extra-ordinary power' (Weber, 1968, p. 225) for the organization and its staff, while, 'in addition to this, bureaucratic organizations, or the holders of power who make use of them, have the tendency to increase their power still further by the knowledge growing out of experience in the service' (ibid.).[1]

Weber's model of a bureaucracy, providing its employees with a bureaucratic career through the grades of the organization, depicts a particular type of organization—what Offe (1976) has termed a 'task-continuous status organization', in which both functional and hierarchical differentiation coincide. As a result of the increasing 'de-naturalization' of the effort required for work through the increasing application of technique to technology, the division of labour has become increasingly specialized. Specialization is defined as 'the increasing *difference* between the requirements operating at one position and those at another position' (Offe, 1976, p. 24). In other words, 'specialization is the non-liquidity of the individual labour investment' (ibid.). A consequence of this increasing specialization of skill is the development of a 'task-discontinuous status organization'. This emerges parallel to the rational-legal hierarchy of office, on the principle of 'functional differentiation' (Dahrendorf, 1965). Offe notes that 'hierarchical differentiation and functional differentiation both produce status systems' which 'in the course of industrial development can become independent of one another' (Offe, 1976, p. 24).

This model of a 'task-discontinuous status organization' has a particular relevance for our discussion of power in organizations. What people bring to bear on their participation in organizations is their special skill or skills (Allen, 1975). Offe (1976) suggests that over a period of time functional differentiation based on skill can produce a 'task-discontinuous status organization' which becomes independent of the authority structure of the organization. I have demonstrated earlier in the chapter that power, in organization theory, has typically been formulated as 'a variance from the structure of formal authority'. A connection between these separate arguments can be constructed.

In the 'task-continuous status organization' there exists a relationship between different positions in the hierarchy 'such that there is a wide area of technical rules to which equal obedience is required from all of the occupants of the positions (in the structure)' (Offe, 1976, p. 25). A superordinate position would differ from a subordinate position 'merely in terms of greater mastery of the rules and greater ability, knowledge and experience in production' (ibid.). The rules that a subordinate must obey become, in their entirety, components of the role definition of a superordinate, and so on, up the hierarchy. Offe (ibid.) typifies this organizational structure as 'the production organization of the small craft workshop, with its triple hierarchical division of master, journeyman and apprentice'. In such a structure, power clearly derives from ownership and control of the means of production and, overlying this, knowledge of the methods of production. This type of organization is not typical of the modern large-scale organization, and presents no particular problems for analysis of power.

The origins of this type of organization lie in the development of different labour processes as landmarks in the history of capitalism, from simple forms of co-operation to the fully socialized labour of the modern organization. These have been investigated extensively by Braverman (1974) and by Palloix (1976), who writes of the principle of co-operation that it

> lies in the *coordination* of labour processes based upon *crafts* ('craft' here being given both a social and a technical definition) processes coordinated under the control of the owner of capital, who takes into his own hands the power to select and design particular use values. This coordination of labour processes based upon crafts reproduces in a modified way the hierarchical productive organization of artisanal production, characterized by the relationship between the master craftsman and journeyman (the

primary relationship) and between apprentice and adult workers (the secondary relationship) (Palloix, 1976, p. 51).

As a further stage in the development of organization structures of social relationships, 'the principle of manufacture amounts to an extension of the principle of simple co-operation, with an initial dissolution of the preceding labour process based upon crafts' (Palloix, 1976, p. 51). With the transition to manufacturing, new forms of work, still based on craft skills, are produced: 'the *artisan* becomes a *worker* with profound ensuing effects on social relationships arising from the process of technical de-qualification and hyper-qualification of labour power within manufacture as a result of the fragmentation of tasks' (p. 52).

This signals the emergence of what Offe (1976) termed the task-discontinuous organization as a social creation, which consisted of the following process, described by Freyssenet as:

1) The beginning of the 'deskilling' of the work of the majority. This is brought about by: reducing the field in which the worker's skills can be used and developed:

    progressively suppressing that part of the worker's activity which consists of preparing and organizing the work in his own way:

    eliminating his understanding of the whole of the labour process and, as a result, eliminating his concrete control of the labour process.

2) The beginning of hyper-qualification of a small majority. At this stage of development, the activities appropriated from the worker (whether by reducing the scope of his work or by taking away his direct control of the organization of his work) are transferred by the capitalist to a small number of wage earners who are themselves divided into different categories and subject to the capitalist's control.

The responsibilities of these groups of workers are:
(a) to systematize the fragmentation of work
(b) to adapt each tool, which previously was used for many purposes, to new narrower uses, in such a way as to increase their efficiency (Freyssenet, 1974, pp. 35–6; cited in Palloix, 1976, p. 52).

The owner of capital, through his ownership of the organization's means of production, is thus able to extend his control over the methods of production, and hence over the producers, by the systematic de-qualification and hyper-qualification of the skills which compose the creativity of the organization.

117

Thus was the type of task-discontinuous organization consciously created.

The type of organizational structure which is more relevant for contemporary analysis is that of the task-discontinuous status organization. In this type of organization the relationship between hierarchically ordered positions is such that the mastery of the technical rules of a subordinate position is basically *not* an essential component of a superordinate position. This is essentially the situation that Hickson *et al.*'s (1971) strategic contingency theory addresses, albeit in a de-hierarchicalized manner. This is a situation of functional differentiation, which Offe describes as one where the 'task areas' of positions 'and the technical knowledge and abilities required for their fulfillment no longer coincide: at any rate there is not the smallest element of the role definition of the lowest member of the organization's status hierarchy which is common to all the other positions' (Offe, 1976, p. 25).

It is the existence of this type of task-discontinuous organization which has been the impetus for those studies by Crozier (1964),[2] Mechanic (1962), etc., into the power of 'lower participants' given by control of uncertainty, because the structure of such an organization

> results in a relationship between 'below' and 'above' such that some of the decisions that have to be made in the lower position are not fully covered by the commands and controls from above—they therefore have to be left to the independent decision of the workers (Offe, 1976, pp. 26–7).

Analysis of the changing formal organization of the military is the example which Offe (1976, p. 27) cites from Simon (1952, pp. 155–94) to demonstrate that there are necessary preconditions for direct, extensive formal control. These are:

> 1. The vertical (hierarchical) differentiation must be relatively underdeveloped, thus allowing the direct communication of orders and direct supervision of their execution.
> 2. The events and processes in the sphere of action have to occur within the field of vision and within hearing distance of the superior authorities.
> 3. Functional differentiation must also be rudimentary, not only must the majority of the actors belong to the same rank in the hierarchy, but also actors of the same rank must fulfil identical functions (Offe, 1976, p. 27).

An extremely important point concerning the analysis of power in organizations flows from these simple preconditions. In the previous chapter we arrived at a definition of power which stressed that it was the ability to exercise control over resources which, when subjects engage in or refrain from practices, produce effects on other subjects; in the instance of organizational analysis, it will be those practices that are the visible structure of social relationships, and changes in these, which are the organization. This power is expressed in organizations through the control of the means and methods of production.

The most extensive and basic form of power is ownership and control of the organization. Zeitlin (1974) demonstrates that a majority (60 per cent) of large USA corporations are controlled by ownership interests, notwithstanding that they are extensively managed by functionaires. Work by Scott and Hughes (1976) and Nyman and Silberston (1977) reveals strikingly similar data for Scotland and for England. Additionally, as Francis (1977, p. 2) argues, recent data suggest 'more structural possibilities for groups of institutions to exercise control' than the theorists of managerialism had argued (e.g. Burnham, 1941). This is suggested by recent research on patterns of interlocking directorships by Levine (1972) for the USA, Scott and Hughes (1976) for Scotland, Stanworth and Giddens (1975) and Whitley (1973) for England.

The growth of firms to the scale of a modern large enterprise does not by itself make redundant the basic model of hierarchical organization of a task-continuous military, which Weber (1968) used as his model for the development of rational-legal bureaucracy as an ideal type. This growth was indeed spectacular and fast, and could be expected to have generated strains and tensions. For instance, in the field of organization characterized by Karpik (1977) as *industrial capitalism*, the development of today's dominant firms was fixed by their growth in the latter half of the nineteenth century and the early years of the twentieth (see Chandler, 1962). Between the years of 1848 and 1873, for instance, the Krupp works in Essen grew from a relatively small (but not by contemporary standards) firm employing only seventy-two workers to one employing almost 12,000 (Ehrenberg, 1906–1909; cited in Hobsbawm, 1975, p. 213). Development of the metallurgical industry was largely consequent upon the rapidity of vertical and horizontal concentration and technological innovation, and occurred at much the same time throughout Europe. Fohlen (1973, p. 60) notes, for instance, that by 1870 the Creusot Foundries in France employed more than half (12,500) of the population of the town. Changes in the size of firms were uneven, occurring not in a random manner, but as markets and technologies developed in the world economy, and under specifically regional constraints and advantages.

Evolution, development and increase in scale of operations presented firms with problems of management which were not evident when the enterprise was still small enough to conform to the model of the preconditions for formal, direct and extensive control. As Hobsbawm (1975, p. 216) comments, 'the basic model of the individually or family-owned and managed enterprise, the patriarchal family autocracy, was increasingly irrelevant to the industries of the second half of the nineteenth century'. While handbooks of management instruction, as Hobsbawm suggests,[3] might recommend, as late as 1868, that 'The best instruction is by word of mouth . . . given by the entrepreneur himself, all-seeing, omnipresent and ever available, whose personal orders are reinforced by the personal example which his employees have constantly before their eyes', this advice was of little value for 'the lords of rail, mine and steel-mill' who 'cannot really have expected to look paternally over their workers' shoulders at all times, and they certainly did not do so' (Hobsbawm, 1975, p. 216). What alternative was there?

> The alternative and complement to instruction was command. But neither the autocracy of the family nor the small-scale operations of craft industry and merchant business provided much guidance for really large capitalist organizations. So, paradoxically, private enterprise in its most unrestricted and anarchic period tended to fall back on the only available models of large scale management, the military and bureaucratic (Hobsbawm, 1975, p. 216).

We have gone almost full circle. In order to control the labour power it has hired—that is, to put it to work most effectively in the creation of surplus value—private enterprise falls back on military organization as a model bureaucracy for controlling the labour army. The importance of Offe's (1976) work, however, is to suggest that this model of control cound not be successful where the organization was a task-discontinuous status organization. And this became increasingly the type of modern organization, in which, as Simon (1952, p. 189) has argued, 'The broader the sphere of discretion left to the subordinate by the orders given him, the more important become those types of influence which do not depend upon the exercise of formal authority'.

Indeed, this disjuncture between the hierarchical and functional organization, under the impact of the incorporation of task-discontinuous skills into its functioning, became a feature of military organization itself:

> historical research highlights the evolution of the military profession as middle-class technicians during the nineteenth century took over the specialized artillery and engineering services while the infantry and to an even greater extent the cavalry remained the domain of the aristocracy. As the simple division of labour gave way to a complex pattern of specialization, the number of ranks increased and the staff officer emerged as a specialist in planning and co-ordination. . . . All of these transformations implied that positions of authority would have to be allocated to persons with demonstrated competence, that is, on the basis of achievement (Janowitz, 1959, p. 10).

The implications of this for an analysis of power in organizations are quite clear. Historically, we can point to power in the organization as something flowing quite 'naturally' from the ownership and control of the means and methods of production. As organizations have grown in size, and become qualitatively differentiated in terms of their specialist skill composition, control through direct ownership, coercion and command—on a primitive military model—becomes less and less feasible or practical. The balance of the bases of power shifts from one side of Gramsci's dual perspective—that of domination by coercion and command—to the other, that of domination by hegemony. Offe (1976, p. 28) puts it thus: 'As both hierarchical and functional differentiation proceeds, the compliance which results from the effects of formal control has to be supplemented by *additional* normative orientations', while Simon (1952, p. 193) says that 'unless a subordinate is himself able to supply most of the premises of a decision, and to synthesize them adequately, the task of supervision becomes hopelessly burdensome'.

These normative orientations, which, following Gramsci, we shall call domination by hegemony, function as both principle and substance of specific organization structures. As principle, they operate at the general bedrock level of mode of production/hegemonic domination as a form of life, as the *ground rule* of domination. Within this general context, they may be seen in substance in the organization as a structure of sedimented selection rules. Conceiving of these as a possible combination, we can develop an abstract mode of rationality of the development of organization structure.

The mode of rationality of the development of the organization structure

This model of the organization derives from an earlier analysis of language-in-use, which treated conversational materials collected in an organization as the surface manifestation of a deeper, underlying mode of rationality. In the context being developed here, the organization structure can be conceived in terms of the selectivity rules which can be analytically constructed as an explanation of its social action and practice (its surface detail, what it does). These rules, collected together, may be conceived of as a mode of rationality (see Table 2).

Table 2 The main types of sedimented selection rules

Types	Examples
Technical rules	Taylorism, as it defines all that it is technically necessary to know at a specific work-place in order to carry out the relevant tasks, particularly in relation to wage systems.
Social-regulative rules	Mayo, and post-Mayo, interventions to repair social solidarity in the organization.
Extra-organizational rules	Effects of other discriminatory orders, e.g. discriminatory practices of racism, sexism.
Strategic rules	Monopoly capitalism: e.g. buying out of raw material suppliers, dealers, outlets, etc.; links to finance capital, mass advertising, securing of favourable state interventions for social consensus or organizational activities, e.g. social contracts and wages and incomes policies, socialized infrastructure costs.

The types of selectivity rules indicated in Table 2 are not mutually exclusive but are found in combinations in specific organizations. Analytically, they are separable, while empirically they may be found coexistent. The schema is neither a necessary nor a sufficient list, but simply an abstract model, which indicates some of the major rule-governed interventions which have been made in the organization of the labour process in the capitalist mode of production.

In the section which follows I wish to illustrate this abstract schema through a possible history. The purpose of this history is to show how the sedimentation has developed at the mediate level of the mode of rationality within the context of the mode of production. The purpose of these sedimented rules, it will be argued, is to maintain control of the labour process. The organization of the labour process thus becomes the site of a specific struggle between labour and capital. Marx, of course, was well aware of this struggle, but he did not develop an analysis of the strategies followed by capital to accommodate and forestall worker resistance. In this connection, it is worth noting Friedman's (1977) observation of the usual tendency for Marxist analyses to distinguish between 'spontaneist' struggles within the labour process—what Lenin (1956) calls 'trade union consciousness'—and the more strategic 'socialist consciousness' arising from conjunctural analysis of 'the sphere of the relations between *all* the various classes and strata and the state and government' (Lenin, 1956, p. 98). As Friedman (1977) also goes on to note, even analyses such as that of Braverman (1974) have missed the element of resistance within the labour movement to the current organization of the labour process. In contrast to this 'fatalist' view (common to Lenin, as well, of course, in his famous equation of Marxism and Taylorism), Friedman cites the work of recent labour historians in America (Montgomery, 1974; Stone, 1973) and in Britain (Hinton, 1973, ch. 2).

Control in organizations

To reiterate what has already been stated: power in organizations derives from control of the means and methods of production. This two-fold resource base allows the possibility of worker control of methods of production within a context in which capital still controls the means of production. It is in such a situation that strategically contingent workers (Hickson *et al.*, 1971) or workers with a degree of control of uncertainty (Crozier, 1964) have a strictly limited potential for a small, minor but relative degree of control over and above that formally granted them. But such marginal elements of control must be seen in the context of the capitalist mode of production.

Within the capitalist mode of production the economy is both the dominant and determinant structural level, over and above the ideological and political levels. Within this economy labour faces capital *individually* as citizen and consumer, while *capital* confronts the individual as that which controls the possibilities of his or her employment. Labour gains short-term, individualistic personal income from the exchange, while capital gains, in return for this labour, control over not only it, but all it makes possible: production, commodities, distribution, technologies, etc. Control over these domains is grounded in the institutions of 'private property' (for early Marxist discussion of which one can consult Engels, 1969), which provide

> a general normative pressure and a potentially vast network of supporters (in formal as well as informal positions) who can be mobilized to protect the existing social and material arrangements. Also, definite 'support structures' are formally organized and charged with the responsibility of preventing disruption of the system: judicial, administrative and police branches of the State. They function both explicitly (by legal directives, e.g. to protect private property and prerogatives of the owners and managers of private property) and implicitly (by a set of assumptions underlying policies and operations with respect to business enterprises) to maintain the position of employers in autonomous private properties and their rights to operate their firms without 'undue interference' from workers, consumers, or the general public. In particular, the police and courts of the capitalist state operate to guarantee that, should ideology and persuasion fail, the structure of socio-economic relations and the configuration of constraints outlined above would be maintained 'by other means': namely, 'legitimized force' (Baumgartner *et al.*, 1977, p. 6).

These constraints are, of course, historically *conditioned*. In a period in which the rate of exploitation of labour and the rate of exploitation of surplus value by capital (which are, of course, opposite sides of the same coin) are in decline, then the type of labour control which is most readily enforced by the power of ownership is compulsion: work on the owner's terms, or no work at all. Increasingly, in industrial and manufacturing organizations these terms became ones in which 'the quality and intensity of the labour are here controlled by the form in which the wages of labour are paid' and so 'supervision is to a considerable extent rendered superfluous. Piece-work rates, therefore, form the groundwork of the modern system of domestic industry . . . and also of a hierarchically organized system of exploitation and subjugation' (Marx, 1974, p. 604). Marx (p. 607) argued 'that piece-wage rates are the form of wages most suitable to the capitalist method of production'. As Hobsbawm (1975, p. 219) summarizes the advantages, they were that piece-wages

> provided a genuine incentive for the worker to intensify his labour and thus raise his productivity, a guarantee against slacking, an automatic device for reducing the wage-bill in times of depression, as well as a convenient method—by the cutting of piece-rates—to reduce labour costs and to prevent wages from rising higher than was thought necessary or proper. It divided workers from one another, since their earnings might vary widely even within the same establishment, or different types of labour might be paid in entirely different ways.

But there were also disadvantages:

> The trouble was that (where it was not already part of tradition) the introduction of piece-work was often resisted, especially by the skilled men, and that it was complex and obscure not only for the workers, but for employers who often had only the haziest idea of what production-norms to set (Hobsbawm, 1975, p. 219).

Frederick Winslow Taylor was to help them with this, and in so doing was to prepare the ground for the development of the task-discontinuous organization in which 'power', in the sense developed by organization theorists, appears on the stage for the first time. Let us be quite clear about this: hitherto, power in the sense of a variance from formal authority/domination (depending on the nature and degree of hegemonic domination, the structure of control in the organization will appear as more or less one of 'authority') was hardly conceivable; organizations which were either small or task-continuous posed no problem of control because they had no unauthorized *structural* sources of power within them. Before we go on to discover what these structural sources of power might be, we shall consider the importance of Taylor's developments in the formation of technical rules as they are organized in relation to payment systems.

Control in organizations: technical rules
Control based on technical rules emerged in the period after 1895, when Taylor's first writing, 'A Piece Rate System, being a step towards partial solution of the labour problem', was read to the American Society of Mechanical Engineers (Sohn-Rethel, 1976, p.

28). This labour problem was that of *control*: how 'to provide a really effective *general* mechanism for keeping labour hard at work' (Hobsbawm, 1975, p. 221). Hitherto, the mechanisms had been fairly simple: the existence of the reserve army of the unemployed and the constant insecurity of employment and the misery of poverty on the negative side, and on the positive side, the existence of 'piece-work'. It had not always been like this: 'In eighteenth-century England workers expected to get a fair day's wage in return for a fair day's work and when there was some dispute about what was "fair" in this context they expected the Justice of the Peace to arbitrate by fixing wages' (Deane, 1973, p. 219). This bargain tended to work in the employers' favour,

> For the buyers in the labour market operated on the principle of
> buying in the cheapest market and selling in the dearest, though
> sometimes ignorant of proper cost accounting methods. But the
> sellers were not normally asking the maximum wage which the
> traffic would bear and offering in return the minimum quantity of
> labour they could get away with. They were trying to earn a decent
> living as human beings. They were perhaps trying to 'better
> themselves'. In brief, though naturally not insensitive to the
> difference between lower and higher wages, they were engaged in
> human life rather than in an economic transaction. . . .
> Increasingly, during our period [1848–75] the wage relationship was
> transformed into a pure market relationship, a cash nexus
> (Hobsbawm, 1975, pp. 222–3, p. 218).

The development of the cash-nexus as the normal form of labour control was assisted by the economic expansion of the period from 1850 to the time of the Great Depression of the 1870s, out of which, as an antidote, Taylorism was to emerge. With this depression the system of the capitalist world economy was fully cemented. The depression was one in which a 'paralysing decline of the rate of profit' was a 'root cause' (Sohn-Rethel, 1976, p. 28), due to the emergence of capitalism on a global, rather than mainly British, scale (Hobsbawm, 1969).

> The post-liberal era was one of international competition between
> rival national economies—the British, the German, the North
> American; a competition sharpened by the difficulties which firms
> within each of these economies now discovered, during the period of
> depression, in making adequate profits (Hobsbawm, 1975, p. 304).

Economic growth developed into economic struggle, on both the domestic and the international front. Internationally, this was the period which saw the emergence of the 'New Imperialism' as an attempt to expand new markets abroad, while at home Taylorism, or 'scientific management', developed as a way of attempting to quicken the rate of exploitation of labour in the production process, through the reorganization of the exchange relationship at work,⁴ manufacturing in part for the untapped domestic high-wage labour market which Taylorism made possible and which the growth of mass-advertising captured and trained (see Ewen, 1976).

Taylor was the founder of 'scientific management', the time and motion study of operations which derives its claim to science from 'accurate and scientific study of unit times' (Taylor, 1903, p. 58). What that technique of scientific management does is 'aim to increase productivity by improving the performance of the workers' (Anastasi, 1964, p. 173) by taking given manual operations and analysing them into their component, smallest and simplest, elements of motion. Its 'scientific standards' of measurement of human labour time derive from the mechanical and technological aspects of the operations being analysed, and, indeed, its operative principle is to measure the unity of labour and machinery in their productive application. This is not a unity of equals, for human power becomes subordinated to mechanical power:

> The tool integrated into the system of machinery becomes a 'machine-tool', a machine which incorporates social relations. Machinery is not neutral because the machine incorporates in its mode of operation the dexterity and the skill of the individual worker who is henceforth deprived of his skill and subordinated, from the point of view of social production, to the machine, which he can only serve, set in motion, and regulate. . . . Capitalist development of machinery in the factory contributes, on the one hand, to a massive 'deskilling' of production workers, together with a loss of autonomy in the reproduction of labour power, and on the other hand to an 'over-skilling' of a small number of workers responsible for innovation, organization, regulation and repair (Palloix, 1976, p. 53).

Hence, as workers responsible for control of the 'methods' of production—the skills of the organization—these latter workers are 'Taylorized' into positions of power-capacity in the formal structure of the organization.

Taylor was an historical agent, rather than an individual subject. The first stages of organizational development in the early phase of the Industrial Revolution were based on a relatively simple application of craft-skills and ingenuity in a task-continuous setting. Those early developments which led to the growth of the textiles, railway and shipbuilding organizations typical of this first phase of British industrial development were scientifically archaic.

> Yet the very scale of the railway, and the transport revolution it inaugurated, made scientific technology more necessary, and the expansion of the world economy increasingly presented industry with strange natural raw materials which required scientific processing for effective use (for example rubber and petroleum). . . . The basic institution of science, the research laboratory—especially the university research laboratory—had also developed between, say, 1790 and 1830. Scientific technology not only became more desirable, but also possible.

> The major technical advances of the second half of the nineteenth century were therefore essentially scientific; that is to say they required at the very least some knowledge of recent developments in pure science for original inventions, a far more consistent process of scientific experiment and testing for their development, and an increasingly close and continuous link between industrialists, technologists and professional scientists and scientific institutions (Hobsbawm, 1969, pp. 172–3).

The fruits of this collaboration were to be found not only in industries based on the development of new sciences of transformation (Karpik, 1977), in which the institutions of the market and the laboratory became fused (e.g. optics, Zeiss; chemistry, Mond; electrical engineering, Edison), but also in the refinement of existing techniques, notably in metallurgy, which, with the development of steel alloys which were sufficiently hard and sharp to cut steel at high mechanical speeds, led to the increasing utilization of machine-tools for mass production (at first for the state in the field of armaments). Mass production requires mass markets, and these were to be found initially in the expanding high-wage economy (because of permanent nineteenth-century US labour shortages) of the USA.

Not only was the labour in short supply, its skills, where they existed, were not prerequisites of production on a mass scale: indeed, skilled labour was not to be encouraged in certain respects, since it was 'the best, soberest, and ablest workers' who were the most likely to form trade unions (Hobsbawm, 1975, p. 221) and hence, because of their *market power*, based on the only *resource* they owned, their *skill*, to bite into the accumulation of surplus-value by organizing for a greater exchange-value. Palloix (1976, p. 57) describes the factors at work in this situation:

> In the U.S. at the end of the 19th Century, the skilled workers, those
> with trade or craft training, together with those immigrants who had
> experience in trades-union and political activities, engaged in a
> political struggle which was widespread enough to form an obstacle
> to the valorization and accumulation of capital. At the same time
> there was arriving from Europe a mass of peasant immigrants who
> could not be incorporated just as they were into the process of
> production. Labour processes therefore had to be modified. On the
> one hand they had to be adapted so as to make possible the
> de-skilling of the 'craft' workers, and on the other hand they had to
> be adapted so as to allow the employment of workers who were
> unskilled, or who could be very easily rendered unskilled.

The remedy for this was to be the analysis and breakdown of human skills, parallel and in addition to the developing machine processes. It was in the metallurgical industry of the USA that these first systematic attempts at *organization* were conducted by Taylor.

With Sohn-Rethel (1976, p. 33) I wish to propose that Taylorism, at least in its own explicit principles, albeit that its particular 'defects' have been criticized and refined (e.g. Barnes and Mundel, 1938; Hecker *et al.*, 1956; Farmer, 1923), forms the basis of the technical control that is the most specific basic type of hegemonic domination in task-discontinuous organizations of all kinds. The stated intention of the recommendations contained in Taylor's main work, 'On the art of cutting metals' (1907), was that control of their labour power be taken out of the hands of workers, in terms of their discretionary knowledge, in order to centralize control within the organization in a few men. The impetus for his work was precisely to counter the discretionary knowledge-power which skilled labourers have in the organizational setting:

> In the fall of 1880, the machinists in the small machine shop of the
> Midvale Steel Company, Philadelphia, most of whom were working
> on piecework in making locomotive tires, car axles, and
> miscellaneous forgings had combined to do only a certain number of
> pieces per day on each type of work. The writer, who was the newly
> appointed foreman of the shop, realized that it was possible for the
> men to do in all cases much more work per day than they were
> accomplishing. He found, however, that his efforts to get the men to
> increase their output were blocked by the fact that his knowledge of
> just what combination of depth of cut, feed, and cutting speed

would in each case do the work in the shortest time, was much less
accurate than that of the machinists who were combined against him
(Taylor, 1906; cited in Sohn-Rethel, 1976, pp. 33–4).

To achieve the knowledge that he required in order 'to get the
men to increase their output', Taylor began his series of
experiments into scientific management, the findings of which were
designed

> to take all the important decisions and planning which vitally affect
> the output of the shop out of the hands of the workmen, and
> centralize them in a few men, each of whom is especially trained in
> the art of making those decisions and in seeing that they are carried
> out, each man having his own particular function in which he is
> supreme, and not interfering with the functions of other men
> (Taylor, 1907, sect. 126; cited in Sohn-Rethel, 1976, p. 34).

Taylor regarded the most important of his experiments as the
development of slide-rules which enable management, without
consultation with the work-force, 'to fix a daily task with a definite
time allowance for each man who is running a machine tool, and to
pay the men a bonus for rapid work' (Taylor, 1907, sect. 51). The
consequence of this was to be the realization of his original
intentions:

> The gain from these slide rules is far greater than that of all the other
> improvements combined, because it accomplishes the original object
> for which in 1880 the experiments were started; i.e., that of taking
> the control of the machine shop out of the hands of the many
> workmen, and placing it completely in the hands of the
> management, thus superseding the 'rule of thumb' by scientific
> control. . . . Under our system the workman is told minutely just
> what he is to do and how he is to do it; and any improvement which
> he makes upon the orders given him is fatal to success (Taylor, 1907,
> sect. 52, 118; cited in Sohn-Rethel, 1976, p. 34).

At the heart of Taylor's recommendations was his realization
that modern capitalism, in its attempt to maintain the long-run
growth of profits, had only been able to do this by increasing the
organic composition of capital in such a way that, as a primary
consideration for maximal profitability, this organic composition
has to be constantly operative in order to produce a sufficient
volume of output. Thus, surplus-value realization depends on the
production and marketing of a constantly high volume of output,
rather than on low wages *per se*. The mode of accumulation of

130

surplus-value has shifted from absolute to relative strategies, and in this situation, as he analysed it in *Shop Management* (1903, pp. 21–2), 'High wages and low labour cost are not only compatible, but are, in the majority of cases, mutually conditional'. This is made possible through the relation of wages to output, which in turn is made possible by the separation of mental and manual labour, such that control of both the means *and* the method of production is vested in mental labour to 'become the instrument of the domination of capital over labour' (Sohn-Rethel, 1976, p. 37).

Taylorism, in modified forms, has become the orthodox doctrine of technical control in contemporary 'industrial capitalism' (Karpik, 1977), based on the high-wages policy. Gramsci (1971, pp. 310–13) understood that the policy of high wages was the 'persuasive' element in the imposition of the hegemonic domination of capital expressed in its generalization and diffusion of new methods of work and production and the creation of a 'new type of worker'. He also was aware of the particular problems created by Taylorism:

> that 'unfortunately' the worker remains a man and even that during his work he thinks more, or at least has greater opportunities for thinking, once he has overcome the crisis of adaption without being eliminated: and not only does the worker think, but the fact that he gets no immediate satisfaction from his work and realizes that they are trying to reduce him to a trained gorilla, can lead him to a train of thought that is far from conformist (Gramsci, 1971, p. 310).

This 'train of thought' is most frequently expressed in either sabotage (see Taylor and Walton, 1971) or in labour turnover (see Dunkerley and Mercer, 1975). It was this latter factor which Gramsci stressed when he observed that

> The instability of the labour force demonstrates that as far as Ford's is concerned the normal conditions of workers' competition for jobs (wage differentials) are effective only to a limited degree. The different level of average wages is not effective, nor is the pressure of the reserve army of the unemployed (Gramsci, 1971, p. 311).

Gramsci (1971, pp. 311–12) goes on to argue that the reasons for this turnover lie in the 'more wearying and exhausting' consumption of labour power under Fordism⁵ than elsewhere. If Fordism is to gain general acceptance as a rational method of organizing production, Gramsci (p. 312) argues that this 'cannot take place through coercion alone, but only through tempering compulsion (self-discipline) with persuasion'. What form might this persuasion take?

Gramsci anticipated that the 'turnover' problem would be curtailed by unemployment. This was indeed the case, but it did not remain so. The hegemonic unity of the compulsion of the reserve army of the unemployed and the persuasion of high wages was to be broken by the fully employed war economy of the Second World War, as an unintended Keynesian intervention. It is at this stage that Elton Mayo becomes significant, for Mayo, just as much as Taylor, was an historical agent.

Control in organizations: social-regulative rules

The individual enterprise is not the overall economy. At the economic level, the capitalist mode of production is characterized by an industrial cycle of the successive acceleration and deceleration of accumulation, as Mandel (1975, ch. 4) argues. The fully employed war economy and the economy of the long post-war boom would pose particular problems for the organization and control of the labour process at the level of the individual enterprise. Specifically, it would withdraw the coercive domination of the reserve army of the unemployed. In these circumstances, we would anticipate that the balance of domination would fall on the hegemonic side of the equation. In this context, it is important to note that it was during the war and as a result of wartime studies, as the introduction by Smith (1975, p. xxv) to *The Social Problems of an Industrial Civilization* makes clear, that the Human Relations Movement of Elton Mayo and his colleagues was born.

Elton Mayo's particular 'genius' was to be an attempt to restore hegemonic domination without resort to the coercive aspect of unemployment, an unavailable strategy during the full employment of the Second World War. His solution was the proposal of persuasion in the guise of new forms of social solidarity to replace those destroyed by the industrial processes of de-skilling and isolation introduced by the combined efforts of Taylorism and Fordism.

Elton Mayo's initial observations of the destruction of social solidarity by the industrial process were born of accident rather than design, by his association (from April 1928) with a series of experiments into variables affecting workers' performance which had been instituted by the management of the Western Electric Co. at their Hawthorne works, in what became known as The Relay Test Assembly Room (see Smith, 1975), but it was Mayo's wartime studies into absenteeism and labour turnover (Mayo, 1975) which directly led to the development of the 'Human Relations School'.[6]

Mayo described the circumstances that led to his investigations as follows:

> Early in 1943 great public concern suddenly became manifest with respect to the phenomenon of so-called 'absenteeism'; it was believed that war production was seriously diminished by casual and wilful absences of workers from their work. Many alleged 'causes' were cited—illness, difficulties of transport, family troubles, shopping problems, and the like. It was also said that larger earnings induced workers to take unjustifiable week-end holidays. When the discussion was at its height—newspapers, Congress, public meetings—we were asked by an official agency to make a study of the situation in three companies in a metal-working industry of great importance to the war. These three companies work almost side by side in a relatively small east coast industrial city. . . . On arrival in the city we found the general alarm about absences to be as great as elsewhere; we were offered a variety of explanations for the occurrence of absences, based on the personal observations of those living and working in the city.
>
> These explanations sometimes came from company officials, sometimes from the workers themselves or their supervisors, sometimes from persons casually encountered. The explanations most frequently offered were that workers were earning a great deal of money; that, by reason of this, they tended to take small excursions in the week-ends; and that there was much conviviality, especially during week-ends. Everyone who gave us such an explanation had one or more stories of actual and verifiable occurrences that illustrated his claim exactly. It was impossible, however, on the basis of these illustrations to decide the comparative incidence or importance of these 'causes' of absenteeism (Mayo, 1975, pp. 78–9).

Mayo also conducted research into the same phenomenon in aircraft plants in Southern California, and both of these studies led him to conclude that the real cause of the problem was the lack of 'well-knit human groups' in the industrial organization. This was a persistent message in Mayo's work, in which he counterposed 'the rabble hypothesis' of economics and administration to the 'doctrine of human co-operation' which he argued had been the civilizing principle of the Christian Church. The 'rabble hypothesis' was what we might otherwise know these days as the doctrine of 'possessive individualism' (Macpherson, 1962), which, as Mayo (1975) correctly observes, has developed from Hobbes to the present day, primarily in the fields of political and economic theory.

He begins his major work on *The Social Problems of an Industrial Civilization* by noting how a number of prominent thinkers—H. G. Wells, Disraeli, Le Play and Durkheim—have made 'the clear demonstration that *collaboration in an industrial society cannot be left to chance*' (Mayo, 1975, p. 8). This analysis is made more pointedly by Mayo when he specifies the necessity of considering this problem in its relevance for administration:

> Every social group, at whatever level of culture, must face and clearly state two perpetual and recurrent problems of administration. It must secure for its individual and group membership:
> (1) The satisfaction of material and economic needs.
> (2) The maintenance of spontaneous co-operation throughout the organization.
> Our administrative methods are all pointed at the materially effective; none, at the maintenance of co-operation. The amazing technical successes of these war years show that we—our engineers—do know how to organize for material efficiency. But problems of absenteeism, labour turnover, 'wildcat' strikes, show that we do not know how to ensure spontaneity of co-operation; that is, teamwork. Indeed, had not the emergency of war been compelling and of personal concern to every worker, it is questionable whether the technicians could have achieved their manifest success. And, now that the urgency is diminished, the outlook for continued co-operation is not good. There is no active administration of the present who does not fear that peace may see a return of social chaos (Mayo, 1975, p. 9).

Mayo presents a bourgeois and humanist critique of scientific management, which, in its insistence on the hegemonic moment, in some respects echoes Gramsci—albeit from a very different political interest. To accept Mayo's way of formulating this problem, however, is to miss 'both the theme of exploitation and that of the reproduction of the hegemonic strata' (Palloix, 1976, p. 63), although in its descriptive particulars the analysis is substantially correct, as indeed it is in recommending that the most effective form of power and control in organizations is that of more hegemonic 'social-regulative rules', rather than the less persuasive and more coercive 'technical rules'.

Mayo observes that, in what Offe (1976) has termed the

'task-continuous' organizations of the craft industries of the nineteenth century,

> The boy was thus apprenticed in some fashion to his life work and his trade, and began to acquire simultaneously technical capacity and the art of communication with his fellows. In the usual case this group changed but little during his apprenticeship. Thus through practice at his trade with the same group of persons, he learned to manipulate the objects with which he worked and to understand the attitudes and ideas of his companions. Both of these are of immense importance to successful living. Dr. Pierre Janet, in fifty years of patient, pedestrian, clinical research, has shown that sanity is an achievement and that the achievement implies for the individual a balanced relation between technical and social skills. Technical skill manifests itself as a capacity to manipulate things in the service of human purposes. *Social skill shows itself as a capacity to receive communications from others, and to respond to the attitudes and ideas of others in such fashion as to promote congenial participation in a common task* (Mayo, 1975, p. 12; my emphasis).

Mayo maintains that the balance between technical and social skills (technical and social-regulative rules) has been lost in the modern world. What was has passed and will not return—'*We have in fact passed beyond that stage of human organization in which effective communication and collaboration were secured by established routines of relationship*' (Mayo, 1975, p. 12). Nor is it any longer 'possible for an industrial society to assume that the technical processes of manufacture will exist unchanged for long in any type of work' (ibid.). The 'task-discontinuous organization', in Offe's (1976) phrase, is now the norm, in which both 'a much higher type of skill is required . . . which is based upon adequate scientific and engineering knowledge and is consequently adaptable or even creative'. But, as Mayo (1975, pp. 12–13) goes on to observe, 'the skill required of the machine-hand has drifted downwards; he has become more of a machine tender and less a mechanic'. While considerable effort has been expended on the development of technical skills (i.e., de-skilling and hyper-skilling), 'no equivalent effort to develop social or collaborative skill has yet appeared to compensate or balance the technical development' (p. 13). What are these social skills? In 'ordinary language', learning 'to be a good fellow', learning 'to get on with' one's fellows, says Mayo (p. 13).[7] More technically, 'adaptive social skills' (p. 29). Adaptive to what? one may enquire. The answer is clear. Mayo says that

I must not be supposed to be arguing for the placing of any
limitation upon scientific advance, technical improvement, or, in
general, change in industrial methods. On the contrary, I am entirely
for technical advancement and the rapid general betterment of
standards of living (Mayo, 1975, p. 28),

and immediately follows this with the by now familiar injunction
about the necessity for 'social skills'. These social skills will help
gain the assent of members of the organization to the orders of its
executives. This process is described by Mayo (p. 45), in a passage
which he cites from Barnard (1938, p. 175), in the following terms:

authority depends upon a co-operative personal attitude of
individuals on the one hand; and the system of communication in the
organization on the other.

Social skills will, and should, be oriented to the achievement of
this, and this can be realized through the establishment of 'teams'
in the social organization of work and 'interviews', the latter as an
instrument designed to aid 'the individual to get rid of useless
emotional complications', 'to associate more easily, more
satisfactorily, with other persons—fellow workers or supervisors—
with whom he is in daily contact' and to develop in the worker a
'desire and capacity to work better with management'.

Mayo's 'hegemonic' answer to the control of labour has been
fully adopted by the most progressive elements in industry in the
contemporary forms of job-enrichment and autonomous work-
groups (Maher, 1971), which are, as Palloix (1976, p. 63) suggests,
'an adaptation of Taylorism and Fordism to new conditions of
struggle in production, with the aim of *preserving* the profitability
of capital, rather than a *radical revolution* of the labour process'.
Palloix defines job-enrichment as

a change in the labour process which calls Taylorism and Fordism
into question in relation to the fragmentation of work. This involves
both the re-grouping of several work operations of the same basic
kind as before, but now with greater variety at each work station
(instead of the very small number of operations at each work station
on a typical assembly line) so as to increase the duration of the
work-unit (from one half to more than fifteen minutes); and also
allowing the workers themselves to monitor their own work (they
take over a limited number of the operations of regulation,
quality-control and maintenance). Job enrichment would lead to the
abolition of the assembly line (Palloix, 1976, p. 63).

Palloix observes that job-enrichment experiments have been conducted in the USA, in large international firms such as Texas Instruments, Polaroid, Corning Glass, IBM, Chrysler, Ford and General Motors (Pignon and Querzola, 1973). In Europe there are such schemes as the well-known Volvo and Saab experiments, and others have been developed in ICI, Philips, Olivetti and Fiat. Such innovations do not challenge the Taylorist division of labour into a hierarchy of mental and manual skills: they are neo-Taylorist rather than anti-Taylorist, and conform strictly to Mayo's (1975) intention not to negate a Taylorist division of labour, but to attempt to preserve it through new forms of 'persuasion' in changed conditions of control.

Increasingly, as Ramsay (1977) has demonstrated, the state has been extremely active in innovating new forms of control through co-determination, worker participation and so on. This is not a novel role for the state to play. The state, as has historically been its role, even in its advocacy of *laissez-faire* policies, has been an active agent intervening in conditions of control in organizations (see Taylor, 1972). In general, the state intervenes in modern organizational processes by establishing a framework in which conflicts between labour and capital can be, depending on political complexion, outlawed or contained (within which range there is an enormous empirical variation). Ramsay (1977) has observed how one social-regulative class of interventions sponsored by the state, that of reforms calling for participation, have been cyclical occurrences, varying with the fortunes of the world economy. At times of full employment and high wages, calls for 'participation' have generally increased. The development of Mayoist strategies during the Second World War may be noted in this context.

In the context of an argument which seeks to distinguish what is distinctive about the Yugoslav system of self-management, Baumgartner *et al.* (1977, p. 27) have observed that participation schemes are

> attempts to blur the social differentiation between capitalists/
> managers and workers by making workers (typically, their trade
> union representatives) into capitalists/managers. Profit
> sharing/ownership participation, in particular, is intended to
> interest workers in the profitability of their enterprise, and thus
> achieve at the aggregate level the same effect in improved
> motivation, attentiveness, and sense of responsibility that job
> enrichment programs try to accomplish at the micro-level
> (Baumgartner *et al.*, 1977, p. 27).

137

These experiments are clearly intended to change the surface structure of power relationships between management and labour whilst leaving the underlying structure of social relationships and hegemony intact. Indeed, what is lost by management hierarchically will be more than gained hegemonically, to the extent that 'interest' is generally attached to the profitability of the enterprise. 'Incorporation' (see Ramsay, 1977) has a long and successful history.

Following Habermas (1976), it is possible to speculate whether or not introduction of a new 'objective' or 'organizing' principle, in the form of demands for a genuine self-management and liberation of work, could introduce a contradiction which might be the locus of new legitimation problems or even crises for organizations? To the extent that these could, as an unanticipated consequence, contradict the existing icon of domination—that of 'private goals of profit maximization' (Habermas, 1976, p. 73)—then, out of a *public* (rather than *exclusive*) participation and the interests of those workers engaged in it, as possible bearers 'of the generalizable interests of the population' (ibid.), there could develop

> the moderation of cyclical economic crises to a permanent crisis that
> appears, on the one hand, as a matter *already* processed
> administratively and, on the other hand, as a movement *not yet*
> adequately controlled administratively (Habermas, 1976, p. 93).

It is because of this that strategies of social-regulative rules, *for capital* rather than for labour, have to be subordinated to a particular form of life and hegemonic domination. That is, the theoretical practice of these rules, the ways in which they are *constituted* in organizational practice, has to be subordinated to the *ground rule* of an 'objective principle' of private interests of profit maximization rather than one of publicly generalizable interests of participation and accountability. If this is not the case, then there exists an objective contradiction of principles which threatens the reproduction of the mode of production at the organizational level.

Control in organizations: extra-organizational rules
Friedman (1977) has suggested that the two strategies which I have termed technical and social-regulative rules may be applied to the labour process not only in different moments of the world economy, but also selectively to different elements in the labour process. Technical rules will tend to be applied to those workers

who are more peripheral to the labour process (less strategically contingent), while social-regulative rules will tend to be applied to those workers who are more central (more strategically contingent) to the labour process. This differential strategy arises as a way of handling inflexibilities generated by contradictions within each intervention into the labour process.

First, Taylorist technical rules could not be applied universally. Not everyone could be de-skilled, nor could everyone be a high-wage labourer. In both spheres, differentials would have to be preserved for the strategy to work. Second, the 'affluent worker' is not necessarily a happy worker (e.g., see Nicholls and Beynon, 1977). Finally, neither is he or she necessarily a very satisfactory worker in a situation which demands flexible workers with a degree of discretion. It is precisely these types of workers, those who are more strategically contingent, that capital will attempt to control through more subtle hegemonic domination: that is, through social-regulative rules as a form of control.

This division of the work force can be carried further through the intervention of *extra-organizational rules*. Those skills which are not strategically contingent—generally those with low status, relatively low pay and low job entrance requirements—can be further distinguished by capital from the rest of the labour process, in order to minimize the possibility of labour's developing a collective consciousness of itself *for* itself. In this way the contradictory possibility that 'participation' may become a collective and liberating catchword is minimized. This is achieved by Taylorizing unstrategic skills in the organization. Because of their low social definition in the labour market, such unstrategic skills will tend to attract the most socially disadvantaged groups in the labour force, those groups which are sexually and racially discriminated against: women and ethnic minorities such as blacks or recent migrants. It has frequently been observed that management will often actively encourage these divisions by overqualifying not only managerial skills, but also other strategically contingent skills, or by locating administration and research tasks only where white male native-born workers can easily get to them (see Friedman, 1977, p. 54; Gordon, 1972, ch. 4; Edwards *et al.*, 1972, chs 8–9; Wolff, 1977; Mackie and Pattullo, 1977; and Berger's (1975) magnificent *A Seventh Man*). There is substantial evidence, as Friedman (1977, p. 54) argues, 'from several countries concerning the more volatile unemployment levels for blacks, immigrants and women', citing Hill *et al.* (1973, pp.

52–4), Edwards *et al.* (1972, chs 8–9) and Castles and Kosack (1973, ch. III) as such evidence.

Control in organizations: strategic rules

Strategic rules are an intervention in the spheres of both production and circulation, while social-regulative and technical rules are an intervention only in the *production* of commodities and not in their circulation. As such, they are a one-sided intervention in commodity production, which necessitates these further forms of intervention of the type of *strategic rules*.

Any organization based on a type of mass production premised on a high concentration and centralization of the organic composition of capital necessarily has to harness its labour-power to its machine-power for the maximum utilizable time, because of the peculiarities of a modern plant economy. The more that such a modern plant is utilized by the organization below its rated capacity, the greater will be the unit cost of its output. Hence, in terms of the production process, economy is achieved, and the greatest surplus *potentially* produced, when maximal production is achieved. But

> between the increase of output and the capacity of the markets no intrinsic correlation exists, since they are governed by economic laws of a heterogeneous nature, the one related to socialized labour, the other by origin to individual labour, the one as a law of the labour process, the other as a law of property relations (Sohn-Rethel, 1976, p. 31).

The consequence of this is that, although the needs of productivity require the use in some instances of social-regulative rules, in order to maintain productivity, these interventions by themselves are sometimes neither necessary nor sufficient.

First, let us consider some occasions in which such interventions are not necessary. One class of such instances indexes a determinate absence from this picture. It can be appreciated that the previous analysis of the need for such strategies holds most of the time for developed market-economy social formations, in which the national proletariat, on the average, will form part of an international labour aristocracy. (Obviously, there will be gross wage differences within any given social formation.) In low-wage, less-developed social formations—the periphery and semi-periphery of the world economy—hegemonic forms of domination will recede in importance. It is for this reason that a large number

(Vernon (1973) estimated it at 187) of US, European and Japanese international firms have established themselves in these more peripheral regions. These enterprises are there precisely because of the reduced cost of the labour process, the possibility of multi-factor supply for core production (in the USA, etc.) and the frequently observed phenomenon of transfer pricing. These firms, as both Karpik (1977) and Adám (1975) have argued, tend to be large technological enterprises. In terms of their control of the labour process, what is not assured by wages which in the local context are considered to be high ones, coupled with a large reserve army of the unemployed, can frequently be assured by the policies of the domestic state. This assured quantity is the existence of a compliant work force asserting relatively little power.

We can now consider the case of organizations primarily operative in the core states of the world economy. For certain types of these organizations, primarily monopoly capitalist organizations, control of the labour process in itself, while it is absolutely necessary, is not sufficient. For these firms such interventions have to be buttressed and supported by strategic rules which intervene in the market. As Sohn-Rethel (1976, p. 32) argues:

> The discrepancy between the new economics of production and the old economics of the market needs to be taken care of by artificial means. It is this that lies at the root of private planning as an indispensable strategy of large-scale modern business. But it is a remedy which does not, of course, eradicate the underlying discrepancy but only allows its further growth. I am inclined to regard the duality of two economics as the root of monopoly capitalism from its very inception. Production that for structural rules cannot, without undue economic loss, obey the rules of the market must necessarily attempt to obtain control of the markets.

As a parallel to intensive control developments (technical, social-regulative and extra-organizational rules), capitalism develops extensive control of the *selectively relevant* features of the market, as constructed by managerial market analysis, simulation models, etc. In addition, organizations will attempt to develop strategies which 'co-opt' the state to their interests.

For capitalist organizations operating on the market, the state exists as a potential source of protection (see McCullough and Shannon, 1977) from the operation of this market. Polanyi (1944) describes two central features of the market system. These are, first, the greater profit accrues to those organizations that possess larger amounts of resources. It is because of this that there is a continual pressure toward monopolization and the creation of privileged access to resources. In addition, however, the market system is dynamic and creates risks and uncertainties for any specific organization, since new areas of demand and new profit opportunities can be continually exploited, often undercutting and disadvantaging existing organization profit centres. Hence, organizations continually attempt to control those contingencies which are strategic for their profit-centred activity, in order to both protect and increase their advantages. This leads organization actors

> to avoid the normal operation of the market whenever it does not maximise their profit. The attempts of these actors to use non-market devices to ensure short-run profits make them turn to the political entities which have, in fact, power to affect the market—the nation states (Wallerstein, 1974b, p. 403).

The general functions of the state have been identified by Mandel (1975, p. 475) as

    (i)   Provision of those general conditions of production which cannot be assured by the private activities of the members of the dominant class.

   (ii)   Repression of any threat to the prevailing mode of production from the dominated classes or particular sections of the dominant classes, by army, police, judiciary and prison-system.

  (iii)   Integration of the dominated classes, to ensure that the ruling ideology of the society remains that of the ruling class, and that consequently the exploited classes accept their own exploitation without the immediate exercise of repression against them.

Engels (1959) conceptualized the state as an ideal total capitalist operating in a sphere in which there are many competing and contradictory claims made upon its budget and policies by different competitive interests, organized as lobbies (representing particular sectional interests), employers' associations and monopolies (e.g. ITT—see Sampson, 1973). Any state tariff, tax, policy, budget devaluation, revaluation, or decision 'affects competition and influences the overall social re-distribution of surplus-value, to the advantage of one or other group of capitalists. All groups of capital are therefore obliged to become politically active, not just to articulate their own views on collective class interests but also to defend their particular interests' (Mandel, 1975, p. 480). These interests tend towards securing increasing favourable state interventions, in the socialization of costs, risks and losses, in an increasing number of organizations (e.g. British Leyland, Rolls-Royce in the UK). Mandel (ibid.) cites some direct examples of this tendency 'as the increasing use of State budgets to cover research and development costs, and of State expenditure to finance or subsidize nuclear power stations, jet aircraft and large industrial projects of every sort. Indirect examples are the provision of cheap raw materials by the nationalization of the particular industries producing them, which thereby make concealed subvention to the private sector. State capital thus acts as a prop for private capital (and in particular for Monopoly Capital)'.

Additionally, the state provides, through guarantees and subsidies, opportunities for the profitable investment of capital in the armaments industry, overseas aid, the environment industry and infrastructural works, as Mandel (1975, p. 485) states. Finally, the state is a capitalist state, structurally, in capitalist societies; it is also staffed overwhelmingly by members of the capitalist class (Milliband, 1969), and it draws its planning information from the capitalist class and its organizations (Mandel, 1975, pp. 496–7). In summary, one could say that the state is not only automatically a source of vital extra-organizational hegemony, it is also the site of a constant battle between different organizations of capital and labour, for control of the resources it has available to it. Successful co-optation of the state can have decisive consequences, as will be argued next.

System contradiction

To borrow a distinction first made by Lockwood (1964) and recently restated by Habermas (1976), no necessary coherence exists between social and system integration. In the sphere of the production of commodities, social integration, in the form of technical, social-regulative and extra-organizational rules, may ensure that no overt crises or conflicts occur, despite the contradictions of private appropriation of socialized production. But this sphere of social integration, while it occurs in production, and thus at the basis of the capitalist system, is the sphere in which crisis manifests itself. Crisis becomes manifest through phenomena such as overproduction, unemployment, short time, wage cuts, etc. This crisis in the organization is generated by contradictions located in the world-economy system of the market. While

143

intensive control is an attempt to maintain social integration, this social integration is itself structurally related to the degree of system integration, with system, rather than social, integration being the determinant of the relation (Parkin, 1976, also makes use of this distinction). Hence, organizations having the structural facility to do so attempt to intervene in the processes of system integration through extensive control.

This may lead to a further, system rather than organization, contradiction, which O'Connor (1973a) has analysed as *The Fiscal Crisis of the State*.

The argument is this. The state in capitalist society must try to fulfil two basic but contradictory functions. These are 'accumulation' and 'legitimization'. On the one hand, the state must try to maintain or create the conditions in which profitable accumulation is possible, but, on the other hand, the state, just like the individual organization, must try to maintain hegemonic domination. Thus it has to maintain 'legitimacy' through retaining the loyalty, apathy or acquiescence of economically exploited and socially oppressed classes, while at the same time it aids their further exploitation. The state cannot afford to neglect the profitable accumulation of certain key organizations: to do so is to risk drying up the source of its own power, the surplus production capacity of the economic system and the taxes drawn from this surplus and the labour that produces it.

We can discuss the process at both the system and organization level.

At the system level,

> although the state has socialized more and more capital costs, the social surplus (including profits) continues to be appropriated privately. Private ownership and control of the means of production permit private businessmen to appropriate a large part of the social surplus themselves. The socialization of costs and the private appropriation of profits create a fiscal crisis or 'structural gap' between state expenditures and state revenues. In other words there is a tendency for state expenditures to increase more rapidly than the means of financing these expenditures (O'Connor, 1973b, p. 82).

This has particular implications at the organization level within those sectors of the world economy which are in decline, such as regions like the United Kingdom. Within the context of the national economy there may be a number of highly strategic and key enterprises. These organizations will be strategic because of their centrality to the processes of accumulation and legitimation.

Let one example suffice to illustrate the issue. British Leyland is central to both the accumulation and legitimation functions of the British state. It was until recently a major source of surplus in the economy, while it still remains a major employer. Precisely because of its centrality to the surplus production capacity of the economy *and* its central legitimation function as a major employer, and because it is the only *national* motor company in the country, the state is in the position of having to subsidize the ailing enterprise on a major and long-term scale. However, although the organization is structurally central (one might even say strategically contingent) to the British economy, it is a peripheral and weak enterprise on the world economy. Hence while the state's intervention, through strategic rules, is absolutely necessary for the domestic economy, in terms of both accumulation and legitimation, it can hardly affect the structurally weak position of the enterprise on the world economy, because of the development of regional dislocations, historically, on a world (rather than local) scale within this economy. The generalization of demands for state intervention in strategic rules, in terms of increasing state subsidies of social capital (accumulation) costs and social expense (legitimation) costs, by individual organizations, while it may lead to stabilization of an individual organization structure, has the potentiality for profound dislocation at the national state structure level, with the likelihood of increasing 'structural gaps' in revenues and expenses. Again, at this level, hegemonic domination becomes imperative in persuading labour as a class to accept the social costs of the restructuring of capital—hence the centrality of the social contract in recent British politics.

These reflections lead me to suggest that the organizational level may yet aid in the precipitation of systemic contradictions. Such contradictions would not only transform the nature of organizations as we know them. They would achieve this transformation in the context of a far more general transformation.

In summary, we may say that the organization will construct itself as the type of organization that it can analytically be conceived to be, by its selectivity concerning those aspects of its position in the world economy that it will attempt to control, or secure control of. At its most selective it will attempt to generalize both its intensive and extensive control, while at its least selective it would be a victim of forces beyond its control—the quaint model of perfectly competitive enterprise. At its most developed we shall be dealing with the organization structures of metropolitan monopoly capitalism and metropolitan states (not necessarily totalitarian—totalitarian states need not necessarily have extensive control, although by definition they will intensify control, e.g., pre-democratized Portugal). The possibilities of selectivity are clearly features of any structure's position and of its historical development within the world economy (see Mandel, 1975, ch. 2).

Implications for analyses of power in organizations

At various stages in this chapter I have attempted to connect my wider argument to an area of specific substantive concern—power in organizations. For instance, I have suggested that it is only with the emergence of task-discontinuous organization that the type of problem which has typically been characterized as 'power in organizations' becomes apparent. This is the existence of unauthorized and informal sources of control over methods of production as a special skill uncontrollable at other levels of the organization. Examples of this are Crozier's (1964) maintenance men or Mechanic's (1962) 'lower participants'. Worked out to its fullest, the logic of this argument leads to the strategic-contingencies position exemplified by Hickson *et al.* (1971). This chapter has suggested some of the specific historical conditions for the applicability of a theory such as 'strategic contingencies', and in so doing raises some questions about the scientific generalizability of such a theory. It suggests the need for a greater historical reflexivity on the part of organization researchers. At the same time, it points towards what may be a more generalizable and adequate explanation of power in organizations.

Power, when it is exercised, is exercised over issues. Given this, then the crucial point is to determine which issues in the world economy (as it is constituted by or impinges upon the organization) are critical for the organization. (This, of course, implies the corollaries of non-criticality and non-issues.) Once we have determined what these are, we can establish which management function(s), group(s) or skill(s), within or without the organization, are responsible for the domain in which they occur. I suggest that a critical issue will be one which affects organizational control of the labour process *within the context of the hegemonic domination of the ground rules* (*the objective organizing principle*) *in which the organization labours.*

This introduction of a structural, contextual *and* analytical analysis into organization research is central to my argument. I am proposing research designs which are sensitive to the suggestion that macro-structural phenomena have an important and differentiating function. In particular I would propose that a critical issue within organizations involved in the immediate reproduction of the capitalist mode of production will be one which affects the ideal of profitability as it is manifested in the organization's mode of rationality. As Pahl and Winkler (1977, p. 115) put it, 'In a capitalist society, effective economic power lies with those who have the ability to conceive and carry through schemes for the profitable allocation of capital.'

The major exercise of formally warranted power in the organization will affect issues that affect the rational functioning of the control of this objective organizing principle. That is, power will be exercised to reassert control. Thus, individual power relations are only the visible tip of a structure of control, hegemony, rule and domination which maintains its effectiveness not so much through overt action, as through its ability to appear to be *the* natural convention. It is only when control slips, assumptions fail, routines lapse and 'problems' appear that the overt exercise of power is necessary. And that is exerted in an attempt to reassert control.

If we were to have a theory of 'significant issues' in the organization, we would implicitly have a theory concerning the functioning of power. The position(s) that 'exercised' power over 'significant issues' would then be the positions that had the effective functioning power to act on issues. (In French and Raven's (1959) terms there would be a disjuncture between formal and expert power.) They would have this ability because they had a specific capacity in a task-discontinuous organization. This capacity would be that of a particular skill (Mulder, 1974, also relates skill to power), specialized to deal with that issue or issues and which was critical to the probability of controlling these issues. (These skills might not exist within the capacity of the labour power that is the organization—in such a case they would have to be hired in either a consulting or employee capacity.) Thus, although everything occurs such as to make it appear that power is either an individual property or a relationship between individuals, it is in fact a social relationship determined by the mediation of the organization's selectivity rules with the 'environment' of the world economy that these constitute and with the critical issues that this selectivity in the service of the hegemonic domination of the objective principle of the organization's functioning engenders. In capitalist organizations these will occur within the reflexive reproduction of specific instances of the capitalistic form of life.

V. L. Allen (1975, p. 218) adds a 'further comment on the relationship between skills and power in a capitalist society'. This is that the 'causal relationship' between them

> is reinforced by the operation of the market mechanism, whereby prices are given to skills according to their scarcity value. Scarcity here is an ideologically based term, contrived to satisfy the ideological needs of the society. But it has a measurable quality, with the consequence that the prices accorded to some skills are determined, within a given range, by the ability of their practitioners to restrict their distribution. The legal and medical professions in many countries have for long endeavoured to maintain a market exclusiveness through a strictly regulated control of the acquisition of their skills. Craft unions in nineteenth-century Britain and the United States recognized that their power in relation to employers depended on control of both the quantity and distribution of craft skills. It is for this reason that unions sought to impose apprenticeship regulations, encourage emigration and resist the spread of skill-diluting mechanized methods. The power to regulate wages is generally least among those with the least demanded skills. As in a market economy there is a premium on scarcity, the **bargaining power derived from skills is distributed in pyramidal** fashion. Other things being equal the commonest skills are at the base and the least common are at the apex. There are, of course, many skills other than occupational or industrial ones. In a capitalist society as a whole, skills, and the power they give rise to, are also distributed in a pyramidal fashion with that of the owners of the means of production at the apex and that of employees distributed hierarchically below (Allen, 1975, p. 219).

The power that employees have is a capacity which is only possible within the framework of hegemonic domination to which they would first have to submit—the possibility of an issue would have to be framed within the dominant theorizing power for it to be ruled admissible. An alternative means of formulating issues might be through radical action which openly challenges the theorizing power of the dominant hegemony (see Allen, 1975, pp. 233–47).

Where the formal structure of domination within the organization and the functioning of power no longer cohere, as a result of the historical development of the organization's skill and selectivity structures, then we could anticipate that unless contradictions persist unchecked—which they very well might—a political process of incorporation into the structure of the organization would be in process, whereby this coherence would be re-established. In this way the administrative functioning of power within the executive's formally conceived structure of domination develops as a dynamic, processual response to changes in the selectivity structure of the organization. This structure of domination is itself a power phenomenon, which I have suggested we might begin to understand through an analysis of the organization's selectivity rules, in the comparative and historical context of the world-economy system. When we compare the degree of inequality of domination which different organizations are able to achieve *vis-à-vis* their competitors and the generalized resource of the state, we are comparing political units within a larger system. These organizations are political unlts of structured selectivity rules which afford differential controls of both an intensive and extensive type, organized around those issues which are critical or significant for that mode or modes of rationality through which the organization operates. This enables us to see organizations as total power phenomena. In this model, there is no sense in splitting off intra- from inter-organizational power, or the organization system from other systems. Intra- and inter-organizational power are features of the same phenomenon: organizational control. Organizational control is not a feature of an isolated organizational system and its environment, but a sedimented structure of selection rules for dealing with one system: the world system.

Notes

Chapter 1   **Method: critical enquiry into concepts?**

1 In some of what follows, I have deliberately followed, with a slight change of detail, Marx's outline of the critical 'method of political economy' (Marx, 1970, pp. 205–14), with the italicized words being Marx's.

2 This formulation is essentially derived from Althusser and Balibar (1968) and Castells (1976), but without recourse to a purely theoretical practice as a way of reconstituting the duality conceived in this, nor to an empiricist conception in which the status of object and subject of enquiry are simply taken for granted. Instead I will argue, in chapter 7, for a model of the organization as a real object of enquiry only inasmuch as it can be empirically comprehended by analysis of the theoretical practices of those subjects who constitute it.

3 Compare the following with Wittgenstein (1968, par. 23).

Chapter 2   **Method and sociological discourse**

1 Clearly, the Reformation of Luther is a contradiction of this. Luther believed that 'the word of God, which teaches full freedom, should not and must not be fettered' (Woolf, 1952, p. 345), and in consequence sought to eliminate all mediation between man and God, which would have implied the dismantling of God's temporal organization, the Church, together with the concomitant rule and domination which comprised the Church's earthly apparatus of coercion and administration. However, we should not forget that Luther was succeeded by Calvin, with the consequence that the former's radical project for the destruction of totalitarian earthly religious authority and the creation of congregational democracy was severely modified by Calvin's re-equipment of the Church with the paraphernalia of practice organized according to the traditional principles of organization: hierarchical control, co-ordination and communication.

2 Nihilism as a philosophical theme has been dealt with most thoroughly by Stanley Rosen (1969). Our treatments diverge considerably, particularly with respect to Wittgenstein (1968) (see Clegg, 1975; 1976).

3 Von Wright (1971, p. 4) discusses the root metaphors.

4 Dahl (1957) can be seen as the almost final flowering of a mechanistic mode of thinking which derives directly from the impact of the Enlightenment on discourse such as that of classical mechanics. At a general level Matson (1964) pursues the lineage from classical mechanics to mechanistic science. Cassirer (1951) enquires into the philosophy of the Enlightenment generally. His second chapter was part of the background reading to this chapter. Elsewhere, in a more general context, I have examined the traces of mechanism still persistent in debates on 'power' (Clegg, 1975, especially ch. 2).

5 The idea of the 'possible society' derives from Wittgenstein (1968) via Blum (1971), and is discussed and used in Clegg (1975). The idea obviously has a considerable affinity with the notions discussed in relation to Zeraffa's (1976) *Fictions* in chapter 1 of this work.

6 Lukes wants to go further than this. He wants to be able to measure not only 'power-effects' but also the concept of 'interests' which Bachrach and Baratz express, albeit 'subjectively'. Lukes is discussed at length in chapter 4.

7 John H. Schaar (1970) makes it quite clear why one might no longer find it easy to discuss 'legitimate authority'.

8 This view finds its methodological advocacy in those scholars who recommend that one should study power 'reputationally', as, for instance, Hunter (1953).

9 Or, as I have put it elsewhere and in a slightly different context:

In attending to the various ways in which theorists have approached and used the concept of power, then, we are attending not only to their definitions and the critiques of these, but to the 'theorizing power' which makes of such definitions and critiques orderly, recognizable and sociological phenomena. The air of authenticity which they wear as plausible scholarship is a manifestation of their mode of production. The actual writing merely re-presents and preserves the deeper possibility of how it is that they are at all possible. Their possibility as features of the sociological enterprise to be discussed, argued, debated and criticized is rooted in their methodical character. They result from the theorists' engagement with method, and are only possible given the theorists' engagement with a tradition of theorizing (Clegg, 1975, pp. 10–11).

Chapter 3   **Power, discourse, myth and fiction**

1 The beginnings of contemporary political science are sharply defined
by three annual conferences on the Science of Politics, which were
reported in the *American Political Science Review*, vols 18–20, for
the years 1924–26. The conferences were based on the view that
objectivity constituted the 'chief hope for the future of the science'; and
their aim was to 'unite those interested in political research' in an attack
'upon the problems of technique and method' (vol. 20, pp. 124–257).
The conference marked the infusion of Watsonian behaviourism and
statistical methods into political science by the leading political
scientists of the day. The participants emphasized, however, that
political science so construed could not 'concern itself with the type,
quality or motives of (political) leadership, as these questions would
involve ethical or philosophical considerations with which the
(participants) felt themselves incompetent to deal' (vol. 19, p. 130). By
sacrificing the core of politics to 'objectivity', American political
science became political science fiction.' (Caton, 1976, fn. 1, p. 155).

2 However, Seaton (1972) argues that the application of Bayes's
Probability Theorem and subjuncture probability (Kyburg and
Smokler, 1964) to power relations is such as to negate Gibson's
strictures on the equivalence of power and causation.

Chapter 6   **Marxist analyses of power and structure**

1 Davidson (1974) establishes, through an analysis of material of Lenin's
which was available to Gramsci in the immediate post-revolutionary
years of 1919–22, that Gramsci did not develop his theory under the
tutelage of Lenin's texts, as Togliatti was later to claim. This refutation
is one instance of the ways in which the contemporary Gramsci has been
produced and reproduced. Both Davidson (1974) and Piccone (1976)
document this extensively.

2 Anderson (1977) delineates two other versions, in the first of which the
pair hegemony/civil society is theorized as superordinate to, and
determinant of, the pair domination/state, and a further version in
which civil society and the state are fused in one pair, civil society/state,
through which hegemony functions, and in which the state assimilates
civil society and becomes conceptually superordinate to it. Anderson
relates this latter version to the development of the concept of
'Ideological State Apparatus' in Althusser (1971), in which formulation
the state all but swallows up the sphere of civil society, with potentially
disastrous results theoretically, as Anderson elaborates.

3 We shall return to this formulation.

4 A major issue for research in the future must be to what extent the 'objective principle' of a particular region within the world capitalist economy, the level at which the next chapter theorizes 'mode of production', affects the mode of rationality and the organizational practice of particular instances within this framework, and what are the contingent variables. Whyte (1973) is a contribution to such analyses.

5 A mode of rationality is a substantive (mode of) rationality (as in Weber, 1968, p. 85) whose 'ultimate ends', in the sense in which I have developed this text, would be given empirically by the reflexive reproduction of a mode of production: a form of life. Also, as Mayntz (1976) stresses, this 'rationality' is more a feature of the procedure whereby decisions are arrived at, rather than of outcomes; it is one of the properties of structures; in terms of subordinate values (within the context of ultimate ends) their 'rationality' will depend on 'joint and simultaneous consideration of several qualitatively different values'; they are constituted rather than triggered by events; and as such they are iterative (see Mayntz, 1976, p. 114).

Chapter 7 **Power, control, structure and organization**

1 Several factors have been discovered which affect the distribution of authority between occupational roles and levels in the hierarchy. The degree of hierarchy varies according to the organization's size (Ingham, 1970) and its technology (Woodward, 1965; Aldrich, 1972). The Aston studies (Pugh and Hickson, 1976) suggest that the organization will be more highly bureaucratized if it is a larger, rather than smaller, organization. Burns and Stalker's (1961) research suggests that the more uniform is the product of the organization, and the slower its rate of technological development, then the greater will be the organization's degree of bureaucratization. These points are gleaned from Martin's (1977) useful summary.

2 For a case study of the ideological role of figures such as Crozier in industrial sociology in France, see Rose (1977).

3 From Kocka (1969, p. 336; quoting from Emmighons, *Allgemeine Gewerbslehre*).

4 It is at this point that our exegesis diverges, yet again, from the conventions of organization theory. Their perspective on the exchange relationship that provides organization with members, or capital with labour, as in March and Simon (1958) or Barnard (1938), is quite

different from that which I am developing here. What I am proposing is a different perspective on 'membership' from that which is typically found in such organization theory formulations as those of March and Simon or Barnard. These theorists stress the conditions under which human and material resources *exchange* for one another, and formulate these conditions in terms of 'inducements' and 'contributions'. If an exchange occurs, the theory proposes that it must be a fair exchange because each person involved in the exchange must have weighed up the inducements and contributions so that they subjectively balance, or are in equilibrium for the induced party. Otherwise, an exchange would not have occurred. This neglects the possibility that a seemingly fair exchange may be underlaid by a prior structure of relations which make inevitable an exchange based on a set of terms which as a rule favour the interests of one party above those of the other(s). It is in this way that Marx (1973b) analyses the relations between labour and capital. This analysis proposes a theoretical understanding of the *social* relations which are entered into in organized employment and production.

Marx argues that fair exchange and profit cannot be synonymous. As Marx (1973b, p. 321) puts it: '*The surplus value which capital has at the end of the production process* . . . signifies . . . that the labour time objectified in the product . . . is greater than that which was present in the original components of capital. This in turn is possible only if the labour objectified in the price of labour is smaller than the living labour time purchased with it'. Raw material and machinery represent fixed amounts of objectified labour time as components of capital. Where the price for labour, the wage, is exactly equal in labour time payments to the amount of labour time the labourer has added to raw material and machinery, 'then the capitalist would merely have exchanged exchange value in one form for exchange value in another. He would not have acted as capital . . . as far as the capitalist is concerned, it has to be a not-exchange. He has to obtain more value than he gives. Looked at from the capitalist's side, the exchange must be only *apparent*; i.e. must belong to an economic category other than exchange, or capital as capital and labour as labour in opposition to it would be impossible' (Marx, 1973b, p. 322).

Such a statement presumes the following specifications. First, that capitalist society is one in which workers 'own' only their 'labour-power', or capacity for labour, while the capitalists own all the means of production, the wage fund for labourers and scarce land. This capacity for labour is regarded as a commodity which, when used in the production process along with the instruments and subjects of production (land and raw materials (Marx, 1954, ch. 7, sect. 2); cited in Bose (1975, p. 76)), produces surplus value which is appropriated by the capitalist. This appropriation represents exploitation (not only in a moral sense) because it involves control of one (class of) person(s) by another. In the long run exploitation exists wherever there is this control (Crocker, 1973), not only where there is positive surplus value (Bose, 1975).

5 Fordism may be defined as Taylorist division of labour, plus the assembly line and a measured day wage, rather than the piece-rate system, which becomes potentially anarchic for capital in the control of labour through industrial relations policies.

6 Smith (1975, p. xxv) summarizes 'Human Relations' thus: 'This school was interdisciplinary in its origins and is generally described as such in its approach, though its underlying concern with the dynamics of group behaviour makes it more properly classed as social-psychological. The chief interests of its members in the industrial setting may be summarized as (i) the relations between productivity and "morale", (ii) the nature of cooperation within work groups and supervisors (especially the effects of participation in decision-making), (iii) the significance of leadership, especially leadership "styles" and procedures in selecting and appraising leaders. The industrial setting for these purposes was normally the "plant", "enterprise", or "organization".'

7 Mayo (1975, pp. 23–4) later informs us that radicalism is a result of social privation, which can be remedied through the development of the appropriate social skills. Recovery, or cure, is indicated by one's former radical views 'vanishing'!

Bibliography

Abell, P. (1975), 'The role of "power" in organization theory: discussion issues', discussion paper presented to the session on Power and Organizations, European Group for Organization Studies (EGOS) Colloquium on Current Issues in Organizational Studies, Bréau-sans-Nappe, France, 3–5 April.

Abell, P. (ed.) (1976), *Organizations as Bargaining and Influence Systems*, London, Heinemann.

Adám, G. (1975), 'Multinational corporations and worldwide sourcing', in H. Radice (ed.), *International Firms and Modern Imperialism*, Harmondsworth, Penguin.

Aldrich, H. (1972), 'Technology and organizational structure: a reexamination of the findings of the Aston group', *Administrative Science Quarterly*, 17, pp. 26–43.

Allen, V. L. (1975), *Social Analysis: A Marxist Alternative*, London, Longman.

Allison, L. (1974), 'The nature of the concept of power', *European Journal of Political Research*, 2, pp. 131–42.

Althusser, L. (1969), *For Marx*, London, Allen Lane, The Penguin Press.

Althusser, L. (1971), *Lenin and Philosophy and Other Essays*, London, New Left Books.

Althusser, L. and Balibar, E. (1968), *Reading Capital*, London, New Left Books.

Anastasi, A. (1964), *Fields of Applied Psychology*, New York, McGraw-Hill.

Anderson, P. (1976), *Considerations on Western Marxism*, London, New Left Books.

Anderson, P. (1977), 'The antinomies of Antonio Gramsci', *New Left Review*, 100, pp. 5–80.

Arendt, H. (1970), *On Violence*, London, Allen Lane, The Penguin Press.

Aristotle (1933), *Metaphysics, Book II*, translated by H. Tredennick, London, Heinemann.

Ayer, A. J. (1966), 'Can there be a private language?', in G. Pitcher (ed.), *Wittgenstein: The Philosophical Investigations*, London, Macmillan, pp. 251–67.

Bachrach, P. and Baratz, M. S. (1962), 'Two faces of power', *American Political Science Review*, 56, pp. 947–52.

Bachrach, P. and Baratz, M. S. (1970), *Power and Poverty: Theory and Practice*, Oxford University Press.

Baldwin, D. A. (1971), 'Money and power', *Journal of Politics*, 33, pp. 578–614.

Ball, T. (1975), 'Models of power: past and present', *Journal of the History of the Behavioural Sciences*, July, pp. 211–22.

Ball, T. (1976), 'Power, causation and explanation', *Polity*, Winter, pp. 189–214.

Barnard, C. (1938), *The Functions of the Executive*, Cambridge, Mass., Harvard University Press.

Barnes, R. M. and Mundel, M. E. (1938), 'Studies of hand motions and rhythm appearing in factory work', *University of Iowa Studies in Engineering*, 12.

Bauman, Z. (1976), *Towards a Critical Sociology*, London, Routledge & Kegan Paul.

Baumgartner, T. *et al*. (1977), 'Work, politics and the structuring of social systems', paper presented to the International Conference on 'Possibilities for the Liberation of Work and Political Power', Dubrovnik, February.

Bennis, W. G., Berkowitz, N., Affinito, M. and Malone, M. (1958), 'Authority, power and the ability to influence', *Human Relations*, XI: 2, pp. 143–56.

Benson, J. K. (1975), 'The interorganizational network as a political economy', *Administrative Science Quarterly*, 20, pp. 229–49.

Berger, J. (1975), *A Seventh Man*, Harmondsworth, Penguin.

Van Den Bergh, G. V. B. (1972), 'On the concept of power and its uses', mimeo.

Black, M. (1965), *Models and Metaphors*, Ithaca, New York, Cornell University Press.

Blais, A. (1974), 'Power and causality', *Quality and Quantity*, 8 pp. 45–64.

Blau, P. M. (1955), *The Dynamics of Bureaucracy*, University of Chicago Press.

Blau, P. M. (1965), 'The comparative study of organizations', *Industrial and Labour Relations Review*, 18, pp. 323–38.

Blau, P. M. and Scott, W. R. (1973), *Formal Organizations: A Comparative Approach*, London, Routledge & Kegan Paul.

Blum, A. (1971), 'Theorizing', in J. D. Douglas (ed.), *Understanding Everyday Life*, London, Routledge & Kegan Paul, pp. 301–19.

Boggs, C. (1976), *Gramsci's Marxism*, London, Pluto Press.

Bose, A. (1971), 'Marx on value, capital and exploitation', *History of Political Economy*, 3: 2, pp. 298–334.

Bose, A. (1975), *Marxian and Post-Marxian Political Economy*, Harmondsworth, Penguin.

Bradshaw, A. (1976), 'A critique of Steven Lukes' *Power: A Radical View*', *Sociology*, X, pp. 121–7.

Braverman, H. (1974), *Labor and Monopoly Capital*, New York, Monthly Review Press.

Burnham, J. (1941), *The Managerial Revolution*, New York, Day.

157

Burns, T. and Stalker, G. M. (1961), *The Management of Innovation*, London, Tavistock.

Butler, R. J. *et al.* **(1974)**, 'Power in the organizational coalition', paper presented at the World Congress of Sociology, Research in Organization's section, Toronto, Canada, August.

Cartwright, D. (ed.) **(1959)**, *Studies in Social Power*, Ann Arbor, University of Michigan Press.

Cassirer, E. (1951), *The Philosophy of the Enlightenment*, Boston, Beacon Press.

Castells, M. (1976), *The Urban Question: A Marxist Approach*, London, Edward Arnold.

Castles, S. and Kosack, G. (1973), *Immigrant Workers and Class Structure in Western Europe*, Oxford University Press.

Catlin, G. E. G. (1927), *The Science and Method of Politics*, New York, Knopf.

Caton, H. P. (1976), 'Politics and political science', *Politics*, XI: 2, pp. 149–55.

Chandler, A. D. (1962), *Strategy and Structure*, Cambridge, Mass., MIT Press.

Child, J. (1972), 'Organizational structure, environment and performance: the role of strategic choice', *Sociology*, 6: 1, pp. 1–22.

Chisholm, R. M. (1966), 'Freedom and action', in K. Lehrer (ed.), *Freedom and Determinism*, New York, Random House.

Clegg, S. (1975), *Power, Rule and Domination: A Critical and Empirical Understanding of Power in Sociological Theory and Organizational Life*, London, Routledge & Kegan Paul.

Clegg, S. (1976), 'Power, theorizing and nihilism', *Theory and Society*, 1: 3, pp. 65–87.

Clegg, S. and Dunkerley, D. (eds) **(1977)**, *Critical Issues in Organizations*, London, Routledge & Kegan Paul.

Cohen, J. (1972), 'Max Weber and the dynamics of rationalized domination', *Telos*, 14, pp. 63–86.

Commoner, B. (1971), *The Closing Circle: Confronting the Environmental Crisis*, New York, Knopf.

Connerton, P. (1976), *Critical Sociology*, Harmondsworth, Penguin.

Cox, G. (1976), 'Intentions, structure and the dissolution of power', paper presented to the EGOS Symposium on Power, Bradford University, 6–7 May.

Crenson, M. A. (1971), *The Un-Politics of Air Pollution: A Study of Non-Decisionmaking in the Cities*, London, Johns Hopkins Press.

Crocker, L. (1973), 'Marx's concept of exploitation', *Social Theory and Practice*, pp. 201–15.

Crozier, M. (1964), *The Bureaucratic Phenomenon*, London, Tavistock.

Crozier, M. (1973), 'The problem of power', *Social Research*, 40: 2, pp. 211–28.

Crozier, M. (1976), 'Comparing structures and comparing games', in G.

Hofstede and M. S. Kassem (eds), *European Contributions to Organization Theory*, Assen/Amsterdam, Van Gorcum.

Cyert, R. M. and March, J. G. (1963), *A Behavioural Theory of the Firm*, Englewood Cliffs, N.J., Prentice-Hall.

Dahl, R. A. (1957), 'The concept of power', *Behavioural Science*, 2, pp. 201–15.

Dahl, R. A. (1961), *Who Governs*, New Haven, Yale University Press.

Dahl, R. A. (1963), *Modern Political Analysis*, Englewood Cliffs, N.J., Prentice-Hall.

Dahl, R. A. (1965), 'Cause and effect in the study of politics', in D. Lerner (ed.), *Cause and Effect*, New York, Free Press, pp. 75–98.

Dahrendorf, R. (1965), *Industrie- und Betriebssoziologie*, Berlin.

Davidson, A. (1974), 'Gramsci and Lenin 1917–1922', *The Socialist Register*.

Deane, P. (1973), 'Great Britain', in C. M. Cipolla (ed.), *The Fontana Economic History of Europe: The Emergence of Industrial Societies.* *1*, London, Fontana, pp. 161–228.

De Crespigny, A. (1968), 'Power and its forms', *Political Studies*, 16, pp. 192–205.

Derrida, J. (1968), *De la Grammatologie*, Paris, Editions de Minuit.

Derrida, J. (1970), 'A note to a footnote in being and time', in F. J. Smith (ed.), *Phenomenology in Perspective*, The Hague, Martinus Nijhoff.

Deutsch, K. W. (1963), *The Nerves of Government*, New York, Free Press.

Deutsch, K. W. (1963), *The Nerves of Government*, New York, Free Press.

Deutsch, K. W. (1968), *The Analysis of International Relations*, Englewood Cliffs, N.J., Prentice-Hall.

Dubin, R. (1957), 'Power and union-management relations', *Administrative Science Quarterly*, 2, pp. 60–81.

Dunkerley, D. and Mercer, G. (1975), 'Labour turnover in the mining industry: a longitudinal case study', mimeo.

Durkheim, E. (1938), *The Rules of Sociological Method*, New York, Free Press.

Edwards, R. C. et al. (1972), *The Capitalist System*, Englewood Cliffs, N.J., Prentice-Hall.

Ehrenberg, R. (1906–9), *Krupp-Studien*, Thünen-Archiv II, Jena.

Eisenstadt, S. N. (1959), 'Bureaucracy, bureaucratization, and debureaucratization', *Administrative Science Quarterly*, 13, pp. 491–9.

Eldridge, J. E. T. and Crombie, A. (1974), *A Sociology of Organizations*, London, Allen & Unwin.

Emery, F. and Thorsrud, E. (1969), *Form and Content in Industrial Democracy*, London, Tavistock.

Emery, F. and Thorsrud, E. (1975), *Democracy at Work*, Canberra, Centre for Continuing Education.

Emmet, D. (1953), 'The concept of power', *Aristotelian Society Proceedings*, 54, pp. 1–26.

159

Engels, F. (1959), *Anti-Dühring: Herr Eugene Dühring's Revolution in Science*, 2nd ed., Moscow, Foreign Languages Publishing House.

Engels, F. (1969), 'The origin of the family, private property and the state', in *Karl Marx and Frederick Engels, Selected Works*, vol. 3, Moscow, Progress Publishers.

Etzioni, A. (1961), *A Comparative Analysis of Complex Organizations*, New York, Free Press.

Eulau, H. (1967), *The Behavioural Persuasion in Politics*, New York, Random House.

Ewen, S. (1976), *Captains of Consciousness: Advertising and the Social Roots of the Consumer Culture*, New York, McGraw-Hill.

Farmer, E. (1923), 'Time and motion study', *Industrial Fatigue Research Board*, report no. 14.

Femia, J. (1975), 'Hegemony and consciousness in the thought of Antonio Gramsci', *Political Studies*, XXIII: 1, pp. 29–48.

Fohlen, C. (1973), 'France 1700–1914', in C. M. Cipolla (ed.), *The Fontana Economic History of Europe: The Emergence of Industrial Societies. 1*, London, Fontana, pp. 7–75.

Foucault, M. (1970), *The Order of Things*, London, Tavistock.

Foucault, M. (1972), *The Archaeology of Knowledge*, London, Tavistock.

Francis, A. (1977), 'Families, firms and finance capital: the development of U.K. industrial firms with particular reference to their ownership and control', revised edition of a paper presented to the EGOS Symposium on Power, Bradford University, May 6–7, 1976.

French, J. R. P. and Raven, B. (1959), 'The bases of social power', in D. Cartwright (ed.), *Studies in Social Power*, Ann Arbor, University of Michigan Press.

Freyssenet, M. (1974), *Le Processus de déqualification—surqualification de la force de travail*, Paris, C. Sill.

Friedman, A. (1977), 'Responsible autonomy versus direct control over the labour process', *Capital and Class*, 1, pp. 43–57.

Friedrich, C. J. (1937), *Constitutional Government and Democracy*, New York, Ginn & Co.

Gallie, W. B. (1955), 'Essentially contested concepts', *Proceedings of the Aristotelian Society*, 56, pp. 167–98.

Gellner, E. (1967), 'The concept of a story', *Ratio*, IX, pp. 49–66.

Gibson, Q. (1971), 'Power', *Philosophy of the Social Sciences*, pp. 101–12.

Giddens, A. (1968), '"Power" in the recent writings of Talcott Parsons', *Sociology*, 2: 3, 257–72.

Giddens, A. (1976), *New Rules of Sociological Method*, London, Hutchinson.

Gilbert, M. (ed.) **(1972),** *The Modern Business Enterprise*, Harmondsworth, Penguin.

160

Glasgow University Media Group (1976), *Bad News*, London, Routledge & Kegan Paul.

Godelier, M. (1970), 'System, structure and contradiction in *Das Kapital*', in M. Lane (ed.), *Structuralism: A Reader*, London, Cape.

Gordon, D. M. (1972), *Theories of Poverty and Underemployment*, Lexington, Mass, D.C. Heath & Co.

Gouldner, A. (1970), *The Coming Crisis of Western Sociology*, London, Heinemann.

Gramsci, A. (1971), *Selections from the Prison Notebooks*, edited and translated by Q. Hoare and G. Nowell-Smith, London, Lawrence & Wishart.

Gramsci, A. (1975), *Letters from Prison*, selected, translated and introduced by L. Lawner, London, Cape.

Habermas, J. (1973), 'A postscript to knowledge and human interests', *Philosophy of the Social Sciences*, 1973, pp. 157–89.

Habermas, J. (1974), *Theory and Practice*, London, Heinemann.

Habermas, J. (1976), *Legitimation Crisis*, translated by T. McCarthy, London, Heinemann.

Harré, R. (1970), 'Powers', *British Journal for the Philosophy of Science*, 21, pp. 81–101.

Hecker, D., Green, D. and Smith, K. U. (1956), 'Dimensional Analysis of motion: X, experimental evaluation of a time-study problem', *Journal of Applied Psychology*, 40, pp. 220–7.

Herbst, P. G. (1962), *Autonomous Group Functioning*, London, Tavistock.

Herbst, P. G. (1974), *Socio-Technical Design*, London, Tavistock.

Hesse, M. B. (1966), *Models and Analogies in Science*, Notre Dame, Indiana, University of Notre Dame Press.

Hickson, D. J., Hinings, C. R., Lee, C. A., Schneck, R. E. and Pennings, J. M. (1971), 'A strategic contingencies theory of intra-organizational power', *Administrative Science Quarterly*, 16: 2, pp. 216–29.

Hill, M. et al. (1973), *Men out of Work*, Cambridge University Press.

Hindess, B. and Hirst, P. Q. (1975), *Pre-Capitalist Modes of Production*, London, Routledge & Kegan Paul.

Hinings, C. R., Hickson, D. J., Pennings, J. M. and Schneck, R. E. (1974), 'Structural conditions of intra-organizational power', *Administrative Science Quarterly*, 20, pp. 327–44.

Hinton, J. (1973), *The First Shop Steward Movement*, London, Allen & Unwin.

Hjelholt, G. (1972), 'Group training in understanding society: the mini-society', *Interpersonal Development*, 3, pp. 140–51.

Hobbes, T. (1839), *The English Works of Thomas Hobbes*, ed. by Sir William Molesworth, 11 vols, London.

Hobbes, T. (1928), *The Elements of Law*, ed. by F. Tönnies, Cambridge University Press.

Bibliography

Hobbes, T. (1962), *Leviathan*, ed. by M. Oakshott, with an introduction by R. S. Peters, London, Collier-Macmillan.

Hobsbawm, E. J. (1969), *Industry and Empire*, vol. 3, from 1750 to the Present Day, of *The Pelican Economic History of Britain*, Harmondsworth, Penguin.

Hobsbawm, E. J. (1975), *The Age of Capital 1848–1875*, London, Weidenfeld & Nicolson.

Horkheimer, M. and Adorno, T. (1947), *Dialektik der Aufklärung*, Amsterdam.

Hunter, F. (1953), *Community Power Structure*, Chapel Hill, University of North Carolina Press.

Hunter, J. F. M. (1971), 'Wittgenstein on meaning and use', in E. D. Klemke (ed.), *Essays on Wittgenstein*, London, University of Illinois Press, pp. 374–93.

Hyman, R. and Fryer, B. (1975), 'Trade unions: sociology and political economy', in J. B. McKinlay (ed.), *Processing People: Cases in Organizational Behaviour*, London, Holt, Rinehart & Winston.

Ingham, G. K. (1970), *Size of Industrial Organization and Worker Behaviour*, Cambridge University Press.

James, B. J. (1964), 'The issue of power', *Public Administration Review*, 24: 1, 47–51.

Janowitz, M. (1959), *Sociology and the Military Establishment*, New York, Russell Sage Foundation.

Jay, M. (1973), *The Dialectical Imagination: A History of the Frankfurt School and the Institute of Social Research 1923–1950*, London, Heinemann.

Jessop, B. (1976), 'Power and contingency', paper presented to the EGOS Symposium on Power, University of Bradford, 6–7 May.

Karpik, L. (1972), 'Les politiques et les logiques d'action de la grande entreprise industrielle', *Sociologie du Travail*, 1, pp. 82–105.

Karpik, L. (1977), 'Technological capitalism', in S. Clegg and D. Dunkerley (eds), *Critical Issues in Organizations*, London, Routledge & Kegan Paul.

Kassem, M. S. (1976a), 'Organization theory: American and European styles', *International Management and Organization*, VI: 3, pp. 46–59.

Kassem, M. S. (1976b), 'Introduction: European versus American organization theories', in G. Hofstede and M. S. Kassem (eds), *European Contributions to Organization Theory*, Assen/Amsterdam, Van Gorcum.

Katz, D. and Kahn, R. L. (1966), *The Social Psychology of Organizations*, New York, Wiley.

Kenny, A. (1975), *Will, Freedom and Power*, Oxford, Blackwell.

Key, V. O., Jr (1964), *Politics, Parties and Pressure Groups*, New York, Crowell.

Kocka, J. (1969), 'Industrielles Management: Konzeptionen und Modelle vor 1914', *Vierteljahrschrift für Sozial- und Wirtschaftsgesch.*, 56/3.

162

Kyburg, H. E. and Smokler, H. E. (eds) **(1964)**, *Studies in Subjective Probability*, New York.

Landsberger, H. A. (1958), *Hawthorne Revisited*, Ithaca, New York, Cornell University Press.

Lassman, P. (1974), 'Phenomenological perspectives in sociology', in J. Rex (ed.), *Approaches to Sociology: An Introduction to Major Trends in British Sociology*, London, Routledge & Kegan Paul.

Lasswell, H. D. and Kaplan, A. (1950), *Power and Society*, New Haven, Yale University Press.

Lawrence, P. R. and Lorsch, J. W. (1967), *Organization and Environment*, Cambridge, Mass., Division of Research, Graduate School of Business Administration, Harvard University.

Lenin, V. I. (1956), *Selected Works*, vol. 11, Moscow, Foreign Languages Publishing House.

Levine, I. H. (1972), 'The sphere of influence', *American Sociological Review*, LVI, pp. 777–87.

Lipsey, R. G. (1963), *An Introduction to Positive Economics*, London, Weidenfeld & Nicolson.

Lockwood, D. (1964), 'Social integration and system integration', in G. K. Zollschan and W. Hirsch (eds), *Explorations in Social Change*, London, Routledge & Kegan Paul.

Luhmann, N. (1976), 'A general theory of organized social systems', in G. Hofstede and M. S. Kassem (eds), *European Contributions to Organization Theory*, Assen/Amsterdam, Van Gorcum.

Lukács, G. (1973), *Theory of the Novel*, Cambridge, Mass., MIT Press.

Lukes, S. (1974), *Power: A Radical View*, London, Macmillan.

Lukes, S. (1976), 'Reply to Bradshaw', *Sociology*, X, pp. 129–32.

McCullough, A. E. and Shannon, M. (1977), 'Organizations and protection', in S. Clegg and D. Dunkerley (eds), *Critical Issues in Organizations*, London, Routledge & Kegan Paul.

Macdonald, K. I. (1976), 'Is "power" essentially contested?', *British Journal of Political Science*, 6: 3, pp. 380–2.

McFarland, A. S. (1969), *Power and Leadership in Pluralist Systems*, University of Stanford Press.

McHugh, P. (1971), 'On the failure of positivism', in J. D. Douglas (ed.), *Understanding Everyday Life: Towards the Reconstruction of Sociological Knowledge*, London, Routledge & Kegan Paul.

MacIntyre, A. (1962), 'A mistake about causality in social science', in P. Laslett and W. G. Runciman (eds), *Philosophy, Politics and Society* (second series), Oxford, Blackwell; New York, Barnes & Noble.

MacIntyre, A. (1971), 'Is a science of comparative politics possible?', in *Against the Self-Images of the Age*, London, Duckworth.

Macpherson, C. B. (1962), *The Political Theory of Possessive Individualism*, Oxford, Clarendon Press.

Macpherson, C. B. (1973), *Democratic Theory, Essays in Retrieval*, Oxford, Clarendon Press.

McQueen, H. (1977), *Australia's Media Monopolies*, Camberwell, Victoria, Widescope.

Mackie, L. and Pattullo, P. (1977), *Women at Work*, London, Tavistock Women's Studies.

Maher, J. R. (1971), *New Perspectives in Job Enrichment*, New York, Van Nostrand Reinhold.

Mandel, E. (1975), *Late Capitalism*, London, New Left Books.

March, J. G. (1955), 'An introduction to the theory and measurement of influence', *American Political Science Review*, 49, pp. 431–51.

March, J. G. and Simon, H. A. (1958), *Organizations*, New York, Wiley.

Marcuse, H. (1964), *One-Dimensional Man*, London, Routledge & Kegan Paul.

Marcuse, H. (1971), 'Industrialisation and capitalism', trans. by K. Morris, in O. Stammer (ed.), *Max Weber and Sociology Today*, Oxford, Blackwell, pp. 133–70.

Martin, R. (1971), 'The concept of power: a critical defence', *British Journal of Sociology*, XXII: 3, pp. 240–56.

Martin, R. (1977), *The Sociology of Power*, London, Routledge & Kegan Paul.

Martins, H. (1974), 'Time and theory in sociology', in J. Rex (ed.), *Approaches to Sociology: An Introduction to Major Trends in British Sociology,* London, Routledge & Kegan Paul.

Marx, K. (1954), *Capital*, vol. 1, Moscow, Foreign Languages Publishing House.

Marx, K. (1962), *Capital*, vol. 3, Moscow, Foreign Languages Publishing House.

Marx, K. (1969), 'The eighteenth brumaire of Louis Bonaparte', in L. S. Feuer (ed.), *Marx and Engels: Basic Writings on Politics and Philosophy*, London, Fontana.

Marx, K. (1970), *A Contribution to the Critique of Political Economy*, Moscow, Progress Publishers.

Marx, K. (1973a), *Economic and Philosophical Manuscripts of 1844*, edited with an introduction by Dirk J. Struik, trans. by M. Milligan, London, Lawrence & Wishart.

Marx, K. (1973b), *Grundrisse: Introduction to the Critique of Political Economy*, trans. and with a foreword by M. Nicolaus, Harmondsworth, Penguin.

Marx, K. (1974), *Capital*, vol. 1, London, Dent, Everyman Library.

Marx, K. and Engels, F. (1965), *The German Ideology*, London, Lawrence & Wishart.

Matson, F. W. (1964), *The Broken Image: Man, Science and Society*, New York, George Brazilier.

Mayntz, R. (1976), 'Conceptual models of organizational decision-making and their application to the policy process', in G. Hofstede and M. S. Kassem (eds), *European Contributions to Organization Theory*, Assen/Amsterdam, Van Gorcum.

Mayntz, R. and Scharpf, F. (1975), *Policy Making in the German Federal Bureaucracy*, Amsterdam, Elsevier.

Mayo, E. (1975), *The Social Problems of an Industrial Civilization*, London, Routledge & Kegan Paul.

Mechanic, D. (1962), 'Sources of power of lower participants in complex organizations', *Administrative Science Quarterly*, 7, pp. 349–64.

Meehan, E. (1967), *Contemporary Political Thought*, Homewood, The Dorsey Press.

Merrington, J. (1972), 'Theory and practice in Gramsci's Marxism', *The Socialist Register*.

Milliband, R. (1969), 'The capitalist state: reply to Nicos Poulantzas', *New Left Review*, 59, pp. 53–60.

Mills, C. W. (1959), *The Causes of World War Three*, London, Secker & Warburg.

Minogue, K. (1959), 'Power in politics', *Political Studies*, 7: 3, pp. 269–83.

Montgomery, D. (1974), 'The new unionism and the transformation of workers' consciousness in America 1909–1922', *Journal of Social History*, vol. 7, 4, pp. 509–29.

Morgenthau, H. J. (1965), *Politics among Nations*, New York, Knopf.

Mulder, M. (1971), 'Power equalization through participation?', *Administrative Science Quarterly*, 16, pp. 31–8.

Mulder, M. (1974), *Power Distance Reduction Tendencies: Problems of Power and Power Relations*, Delft, Foundation for Business Sciences.

Myres, J. L. (1927), *The Political Ideas of the Greeks*, New York, Abingdon Press.

Nicholls, T. and Beynon, H. (1977), *Living with Capitalism*, London, Routledge & Kegan Paul.

Nyman, S. and Silberston, Z. A. (1978), 'The ownership and control of industry', *Oxford Economic Papers*, 30, 1, pp. 74–101.

O'Connor, J. (1973b), 'Summary of the theory of the fiscal crisis', Martin's Press.

O'Connor, D. (1973b), 'Summary of the theory of the fiscal crisis', *Kapitalistate*, 1, pp. 79–83.

Offe, C. (1972), 'Political authority and class structures—an analysis of capitalist societies', *International Journal of Sociology*, 2: 1, pp. 73–108.

Offe, C. (1976), *Industry and Inequality*, London, Edward Arnold.

Oppenheim, F. E. (1961), *Dimensions of Freedom*, New York, St. Martin's Press.

Pahl, R. E. and Winkler, J. T. (1974), 'The economic élite: theory and practice', in P. Stanworth and A. Giddens (eds), *Élites and Power in British Society*, Cambridge University Press.

Palloix, C. (1976), 'The labour process: from Fordism to neo-Fordism', in *C.S.E. Pamphlet no. 1, The Labour Process and Class Struggle*, London, stage 1, pp. 46–67.

Parkin, F. (1976), 'System contradiction and political transformation', in

T. R. Burns and W. Buckley (eds), *Power and Control: Social Structures and Their Transformation*, London, Sage.

Parry, G. and Morris, P. (1974), 'When is a decision not a decision?', in I. Crewe (ed.), *British Political Sociology Yearbook: Elites in Western Democracy*, vol. 1, London, Croom Helm.

Parsons, T. (1957), 'The distribution of power in American society', *World Politics*, 10, pp. 123–43.

Parsons, T. (1963a), 'On the concept of influence', *Public Opinion Quarterly*, 27, pp. 37–62.

Parsons, T. (1963b), 'On the concept of political power', *Proceedings of the American Philosophical Society*, 107, pp. 232–62.

Parsons, T. (1967), *Sociological Theory and Modern Society*, New York, Free Press.

Partridge, P. H. (1962), 'Some notes on the concept of power', *Political Studies*, 11: 3, pp. 107–25.

Passigli, S. (1973), 'On power, its intensity and distribution', *European Journal of Political Research*, 1, pp. 163–77.

Petrie, H. (1971), 'Science and metaphysics: a Wittgenstein interpretation', in E. D. Klemke (ed.), *Essays on Wittgenstein*, London University Press, pp. 138–72.

Piccone, P. (1976), 'Gramsci's Marxism: beyond Lenin and Togliatti', *Theory and Society*, 3: 4, pp. 485–512.

Pickvance, C. (ed.) (1976), *Urban Sociology: Critical Essays*, London, Tavistock.

Pignon, D. and Querzola, J. (1973), 'Dictature et démocratie dans la production', in A. Gorz (ed.), *Critique de la division du travail*, Paris, Seuil, pp. 103–59.

Pitkin, H. F. (1972), *Wittgenstein and Justice: On the Significance of Ludwig Wittgenstein for Social and Political Thought*, London, University of California Press.

Polanyi, K. (1944), *The Great Transformation*, Boston, Beacon Press.

Polsby, N. W. (1959), 'The sociology of community power: a reassessment', *Social Forces*, 37: March, pp. 232–6.

Polsby, N. (1963), *Community Power and Political Theory*, New Haven, Yale University Press.

Poulantzas, N. (1973), *Political Power and Social Classes*, London, New Left Books.

Pugh, D. S. and Hickson, D. J. (1976), *Organizational Structure in its Context: The Aston Programme 1*, London, Saxon House.

Ramsay, H. (1977), 'Cycles of control: worker participation in sociological and historical perspective', *Sociology*, 11: 3, pp. 481–506.

Rice, A. K. (1963), *The Enterprise and Its Environment*, London, Tavistock.

Riker, W. H. (1964), 'Some ambiguities in the notion of power', *American Political Science Review*, 58: June, pp. 341–9.

Roethlisberger, F. and Dickson, W. J. (1939), *Management and the Worker*, Cambridge, Mass., Harvard University Press.

Rose, M. (1977), 'Service of power and sociology in modern France: the case of *Sociologie du Travail*', paper presented to the British Sociological Association Annual Conference, Sheffield.

Rosen, S. (1969), *Nihilism: A Philosophical Essay*, New Haven, Yale University Press.

Russell, B. (1938), *Power: A New Social Analysis*, London, Allen & Unwin.

Ryle, G. (1949), *The Concept of Mind*, London, Hutchinson.

Sacks, H. (1972), 'An initial investigation of the usability of conversational data for doing sociology', in D. Sudnow (ed.), *Studies in Social Interaction*, New York, Free Press, pp. 31–74.

Salamini, L. (1974), 'Gramsci and the Marxist sociology of knowledge: an analysis of hegemony—ideology—knowledge', *Sociological Quarterly*, 15: 3, pp. 359–80.

Salamini, L. (1975), 'The specificity of Marxist sociology in Gramsci's theory', *Sociological Quarterly*, 16: 1, pp. 65–86.

Sallach, D. (1974), 'Class domination and ideological hegemony', *Sociological Quarterly*, 15, pp. 38–50.

Sampson, A. (1973), *The Sovereign State—ITT*, Hardmondsworth, Penguin.

Schaar, J. H. (1970), 'Legitimacy in the modern state', in P. Green and S. Levinson (eds), *Power and Community: Dissenting Essays in Political Science*, New York, Pantheon Books.

Schattschneider, E. E. (1960), *The Semi-Sovereign People: A Realist's View of Democracy in America*, New York, Holt, Rinehart & Winston.

Schroyer, T. (1972), 'Marx's theory of the crisis', *Telos*, 14, pp. 106–25.

Schutz, A. (1967), *The Phenomenology of the Social World*, trans. by G. Walsh and F. Lehnert, Evanston, Ill., Northwestern University Press.

Scott, J. and Hughes, M. (1976), 'Ownership and control in a satellite economy: a discussion from Scottish data', *Sociology*, 10, 1, pp. 21–41.

Seaton, S. L. (1972), 'Re-power', *Philosophy of the Social Sciences*, 2: 4, pp. 309–15.

Sensat, J., Jr. and Constantine, G. (1975), 'A critique of the foundations of utility theory', *Science and Society*, XXXIX: 2, pp. 157–79.

Silverman, D. (1970), *The Theory of Organizations*, London, Heinemann.

Silverman, D. (1974), 'Speaking seriously' (Parts one and two), *Theory and Society*, vol. 1, 1, pp. 1–17; vol. 1, 3, pp. 341–59.

Simmel, G. (1969), 'The dyad and the triad', in L. A. Coser and B. Rosenberg (eds), *Sociological Theory: A Book of Readings*, London, Collier-Macmillan, pp. 59–68.

167

Simmel, G. (1971), *On Individuality and Social Forms,* edited and with an introduction by H. Woolf, London, Collier-Macmillan.

Simon, H. A. (1952), 'Decision making and administrative organization', in R. K. Merton (ed.), *Reader in Bureaucracy,* Chicago, Free Press.

Simon, H. A. (1957), *Models of Man,* New York, Wiley.

Smith, J. H. (1975), 'The significance of Elton Mayo', foreword to the 1975 edition of E. Mayo, *The Social Problems of an Industrial Civilization,* London, Routledge & Kegan Paul.

Sohn-Rethel, A. (1976), 'The dual economics of transition', in *C.S.E. Pamphlet no. 1, The Labour Process and Class Strategies,* London, Stage 1, pp. 26–45.

Stanworth, P. and Giddens, A. (1975), 'The modern corporate economy: interlocking directorships in Britain 1906–1970', *Sociological Review,* 23, pp. 5–28.

Stogdill, R. M. (1971), 'Dimensions of organization theory', in J. D. Thompson and V. Vroom (eds), *Organizational Design and Research,* University of Pittsburgh Press.

Stone, K. (1974), 'The origin of job structures in the steel industry', *Review of Radical Political Economics,* 6, pp. 113–73.

Tannenbaum, A. S. (1968), *Control in Organizations,* New York, McGraw-Hill.

Taylor, A. J. (1972), *Laissez-faire and State Intervention in Nineteenth-Century Britain,* London, Macmillan.

Taylor, F. W. (1895), 'A piece rate system, being a step towards partial solution of the labour problem', paper read to the American Society of Mechanical Engineers.

Taylor, F. W. (1903), *Shop Management,* re-published in *Scientific Management,* New York, Harper (1947).

Taylor, F. W. (1907), 'On the art of cutting metals', *Transactions of the American Society of Mechanical Engineers,* 28.

Taylor, L. and Walton, P. (1971), 'Industrial sabotage: motives and meanings', in S. Cohen (ed.), *Images of Deviance,* Harmondsworth, Penguin.

Thompson, J. D. (1956), 'Authority and power in "identical" organizations', *American Journal of Sociology,* LXII, pp. 290–301.

Thompson, J. D. (1967), *Organizations in Action,* New York, McGraw-Hill.

Udy, S. H., Jr. (1959), 'Bureaucracy and rationality in Weber's theory', *American Sociological Review,* 24, pp. 761–5.

Urry, J. and Wakeford, J. (eds) **(1973),** *Power in Britain: Sociological Readings,* London, Heinemann.

Vernon, R. (1973), *Sovereignty at Bay: The Multi-National Spread of U.S. Enterprise,* Harmondsworth, Penguin.

Walker, C. R. and Guest, R. H. (1952), *The Man on the Assembly Line,* Cambridge, Mass., Harvard University Press.

Wallerstein, I. (1974a), *The Modern World System: Capitalist Agriculture* *and the Origins of the European World Economy in the Sixteenth Century*, London, Academic Press.

Wallerstein, I. (1974b), 'The rise and future demise of the world capitalist system: concepts for comparative analysis', *Comparative Studies in Society and History*, 16, pp. 387–415.

Wallerstein, I. (1976a), 'A world system perspective on the social sciences', *British Journal of Sociology*, 27: 3, pp. 343–53.

Wallerstein, I. (1976b), 'Semi-peripheral countries and the contemporary world crisis', *Theory and Society*, 3: 4, pp. 461–83.

Walter, E. V. (1964), 'Power and violence', *American Political Science Review*, 58: 2, pp. 350–60.

Walton, J. (1966), 'Discipline, method and community power: a note on the sociology of knowledge', *American Sociological Review*, 31, pp. 684–9.

Wassenberg, A. (1977), 'The powerlessness of organization theory', in S. Clegg and D. Dunkerley (eds), *Critical Issues in Organizations*, London, Routledge & Kegan Paul.

Weber, M. (1947), *The Theory of Social and Economic Organization*, translated by T. Parsons and A. M. Henderson, with an introduction by T. Parsons, Chicago, Free Press.

Weber, M. (1948), *From Max Weber: Essays in Sociology*, translated, edited and with an introduction by H. H. Gerth and C. Wright Mills, London, Routledge & Kegan Paul.

Weber, M. (1952), 'The essentials of bureaucratic organization: an ideal type construction' in R. Merton *et al.*, *Reader in Bureaucracy*, Chicago, New Press, pp. 18–27.

Weber, M. (1965), *The Sociology of Religion*, London, Methuen.

Weber, M. (1968), *Economy and Society: An Outline of Interpretive Sociology*, edited and with an introduction by G. Roth and C. Wittich, New York, Bedminster Press.

Weick, K. E. (1969), *The Social Psychology of Organizing*, Reading, Mass., Addison-Wesley.

Westergaard, J. and Resler, H. (1975), *Class in a Capitalist Society: A Study of Contemporary Britain*, Harmondsworth, Penguin.

White, D. M. (1971a), 'Power and intention', *American Political Science Review*, LXV, pp. 749–59.

White, D. M. (1971b), 'The problem of power', *British Journal of Political Science*, 2, pp. 479–90.

Whitehead, T. N. (1938), *The Industrial Worker*, Cambridge, Mass., Harvard University Press.

Whitley, R. (1973), 'Commonalities and connections among directors of large financial institutions', *Sociological Review*, 21, pp. 613–32.

Whyte, M. K. (1973), 'Bureaucracy and modernization in China: the Maoist critique', *American Sociological Review*, 38: 2, pp. 149–63.

Williams, G. (1960), 'The concept of "egemonia" in the thought of

Antonio Gramsci; some notes on interpretation', *Journal of the History of Ideas*, 21: 4, pp. 586–99.

Winch, P. (1958), *The Idea of a Social Science and its Relation to Philosophy*, London, Routledge & Kegan Paul.

Wittgenstein, L. (1968), *Philosophical Investigations*, Oxford, Blackwell.

Wolff, J. (1977), 'Women in organizations', in S. Clegg and D. Dunkerley (eds), *Critical Issues in Organizations*, London, Routledge & Kegan Paul.

Wolin, S. S. (1960), *Politics and Vision: Continuity and Innovation in Western Political Thought*, Boston, Little, Brown.

Woodward, J. (1965), *Industrial Organization: Theory and Practice*, Oxford University Press.

Woolf, B. L. (ed.) (1952), *Reformation Writings of Martin Luther*, London, Lutterworth.

von Wright, G. H. (1971), *Explanation and Understanding*, London, Routledge & Kegan Paul.

Wrong, D. H. (1968), 'Some problems in defining social powers', *American Journal of Sociology*, 73: 6, pp. 673–81.

Zeitlin, M. (1974), 'Corporate ownership and control: the large corporations and the capitalist class', *American Journal of Sociology*, 79: 5, pp. 1073–1119.

Zeraffa, M. (1976), *Fictions: The Novel and Social Reality*, Harmondsworth, Peregrine.

Index